I have theological and philosophical presuppositions about life. I believe things go better with Jesus. I think I made a smart move when I said, "Yes, Lord." I think I make a smart move every time I say, "Yes, Lord." Don't you? It's better to be a Christian. I was going to hell with that other thing, but I'm on my way to heaven now. I don't deserve it, but I got my ticket paid for by somebody else. My reservations are prepaid, too, they tell me. I've been reading the Book! I have to remind myself of that every now and then. I get kind of gloomy and hurting, and a lot of things hurt in my life. Have you noticed that? Today has been a particularly difficult day for me, emotionally, so I had to get alone and remind myself of who I am and where I am going. I'm going to a better place. This is not it; so don't cling to it so desperately. This is just the rehearsal; the play is coming. This is just the practice; the game is later on. This is the preparation and the real thing and the real Person is coming to get you soon. So, in the meantime, let's just do what we can to bless Him since He paid the whole tab anyway.

John Wimber, November 1996

The Way In Is the Way On

JOHN WIMBER'S TEACHINGS AND
WRITINGS ON LIFE IN CHRIST

The Way In Is the Way On

JOHN WIMBER'S TEACHINGS AND
WRITINGS ON LIFE IN CHRIST

John Wimber

ampelōn
PUBLISHING

Atlanta, GA

The Way In Is the Way On
Copyright ©2006 by Christy Wimber

ISBN: 0-9748825-7-7
Printed in the United States of America
Requests for information should be addressed to:
Ampelon Publishing
6920 Jimmy Carter Blvd., Ste. 200
Norcross, GA 30071

To order other Ampelon Publishing products, visit us on the web at:
www.ampelonpublishing.com

Cover & inside design: Lisa Dyches — cartwheelstudios.com

Printed on 10% post-consumer recycled paper

Acknowledgements

Thank you to all of you that have taken the time to contribute to the book, especially Don Williams, and to Carol for the many times I tracked you down to ask you the why and how of things. I'm sorry ... I just never go away!

— Christy Wimber

CONTENTS

Introduction

S ince John's passing, it has been important to Sean and ~~I~~ *me* that we make sure his teachings and materials are kept up and made available. Honestly, it was really Sean that was so adamant to make sure everything was and is done right. Our heritage and foundation that we have in the Vineyard can be so easily lost, and we believe it's most important that we do our best to make sure we have things in "lasting order" so to speak for the generations to come.

Therefore, this book, *The Way In is the Way On,* is a collection of writings and teachings, taken from various settings, as well as stories you may be unaware of. There is so much to share, so much insight and values the Lord gave John over the years. We pray it continues to bless and encourage you, not just as reading material, but to inspire and challenge you to "go on with the Lord" in whatever group, church, or people the Lord has entrusted you to bless.

At the end of the day, if it stirs you to Christ and His Kingdom, then John's desire to see that happen continues. It has been a privilege to share in the opportunity.

— Christy Wimber

Foreword

In terms of spiritual impact on the global Church, it is without question that John Wimber was one of the most pivotal instruments in the hands of the Holy Spirit during the last two decades of the 20th century. Now, early in this new century, it is remarkable timely that his written works be spread, notably when the Church is at risk of spending more time *entertaining* than *equipping* the saints. At the moment, we are highly vulnerable to a fixation with technological savvy or "cool" communication being substituted for the Spirit's power in our lives, and our pursuing a lifestyle that incarnates Jesus' ministry and power through disciples. I'm sure Jesus doesn't want that, and accordingly, neither would John. If John Wimber wanted anything, it was to "do ministry" like Jesus would.

John Wimber was my friend—a good friend; our mutual trust and respect for one another was very obvious to those who knew either of us. John and I first met in the mid-1970s when he would often visit our midweek services at The Church On The Way. The revival grace of God visiting our then-young congregation appealed to John. I recall observing his presence among those worshipping—evaluating, assessing, welcoming truth that seemed to be complementing those deep stirrings God had already begun bringing about in his own soul. It would not be long after that time that his work at the Fuller Institute, and then his classes with Pete Wagner at Fuller Seminary, began to shake up the status quo among traditional evangelicals.

That John acknowledged me as a partner at any dimension in his own journey as a leader is among the warmest compliments and highest affirmations I've ever received. We shared three spiritual passions. The *first* was for Jesus Himself, for He is the Fountainhead of all that flows of the light, love and power of God into our world. The *second*, for the ministry of "the Kingdom of

God"—the term Jesus used as far more than a slogan term for generic spirituality. It was, and is, that term for "the gospel" as Jesus means it to be ministered to the world (Matthew 24:14); a phrase encompassing all the dynamic traits of Christ's ministry where God's invading grace and goodness penetrate our present moment. *Third*, John and I shared (and if here he would continue as I seek to) a passionate pursuit for cultivating believers as Kingdom agents—as disciples filled with the Holy Spirit and renewed in Christ to receive and spread His saving, healing, delivering power, thus functioning as ordinary people in the Name of their extraordinary Lord.

Such "cultivating" of believers essentially calls for leaders who, themselves, are discipled in those simple values manifest in the New Testament Church; leaders who in turn *truly* disciple his or her flock to "be the living Jesus" in their world. And thus you can understand my delight in seeing John Wimber's writings prepared for even wider distribution. For these are tools which not only teach God's Word, but which summon and train His people in ways that will see His Word spoken and spread in the way Paul described it: "...Not with persuasive words of human wisdom, but in the demonstration of the Spirit and of power" (1 Corinthians 2:1-5).

It is the Church's heritage to experience and exercise that ministry. And it's a broken world's only real hope.

Jack W. Hayford
Founding Pastor, The Church On The Way
Chancellor, The King's College and Seminary
President, International Foursquare Church

One

What Does God Want from His Servants?

"INSTEAD OF FOCUSING ON THE GREAT MEN OF GOD,
I PREFER TO FOCUS ON THE GREAT GOD OF MEN."

I always told John that with his head and my body, we would have gone a long way. John had a terrible body with angina, cancer, stroke, and heart trouble.

Let me give you an idea of who John really was. Early on, John was a Quaker when he made Christ his Savior and became a disciple of Jesus. One day when John was about to speak at a family camp called "Quaker Meadow," the camp director told John there was a lady at the camp that had a prophetic gifting and she had a "word" for him. Well, in those days we didn't really know what personal prophecy was, so John met with the lady and her pastor. She sat before John and just cried. Finally he said, "Would you stop crying and tell me what you have from the Lord? She said, "That was it. The Lord is crying over you." Then she said, "When are you going to take your place? God has made you a viceroy to the nations."

Well, the only thing we knew about viceroys was that it was a brand of cigarette. So, honestly he couldn't figure it all out. But his wife, Carol, being the studious person she is looked it up in the dictionary. She had an idea of what God was going to do through John, but this term "viceroy" took it outside the United States to the nations.

I observed John as a friend, co-worker, and family member. He said time after time, "All I'm trying to do is read the book and do what it tells me to do." John had this practical way of thinking in all that he did. I could tell you story after story such as this. But the great thing about John is that he knew who he was. I remember one time when he heard about a gentleman whom he led to the Lord years prior that now lived about 20 miles from John. John heard he had fallen away from the Lord and wasn't doing well. So, he drove out to see the man and talk with him. The man repented and began to follow Jesus once again. That is amazing to me. Here is this man on magazine covers and on TV, and he is concerned about this one man who is not walking with the Lord.

John never understood why people marveled and wanted to talk with him. The simple fact is that John wanted to follow Jesus and do whatever God put on his heart. He wasn't just a "fat man going to heaven," he was a "saxophone playing fat man on his way to heaven."

[Taken from John Wimber's Memorial service, 1997]

Bob Fulton and his wife Penny have been involved with the Vineyard since the beginning stages. They are currently at the Anaheim Vineyard doing missions and leading young adult Bible studies.

———————◆———————

One fine summer day I lost it. I decided I'd had enough, and I told God all about it. I had been working for weeks without a break, doing all the things that pastors do: ministering to people, preaching, preparing to preach, answering the phone ten times an hour, doing the administrative work I hated. And this was my day off. It was a beautiful day, and my wife, Carol, and I were getting ready to go to the beach and then we were going to go out to dinner. I thought I'd like to eat Mexican that night.

Then the phone rang. Reluctantly, I picked it up. It was one of those people in the church who I usually tried to avoid. When she came in one door, I would head out the other—if I could. This time I couldn't. She had some bad trouble in her life that I simply had to deal with. Not tomorrow. Not the next day. Now. On my day off.

Outwardly, I reassured the woman in my most sonorous pastoral voice and asked for directions to her house. Inwardly, I was furious. I hung up the phone and stormed out the back door of my house. I looked up at the sky. I didn't exactly shake my fist at God, but I threw my hands up in the air, palms forward, like an Italian merchant who had just taken delivery of a shipment of damaged goods.

"Who do you think you are?" I roared!

Lightning didn't strike me dead, although I probably deserved to die for my impertinence. I spent the next two days repenting for my sin. God was God. I was a creature, created to do His bidding.

During this time of repentance, the Lord led me to a Scripture passage that had long puzzled me. It was Luke 17:7-10. Jesus is teaching the disciples about faith, forgiveness, and repentance. Suddenly, He shifts gears and starts talking about being servants.

"Say you have a servant," He tells His disciples. "The two of you are out all day working in the fields of tending the flocks and at the end of the days, the two of you return to the house, dirty, tired and hungry.

"Will you say to him, 'Come at once and sit down at the table'"? asked Jesus.

The question is obviously rhetorical. Of course, the master wouldn't tell the servant to sit down at the table. Jesus continues.

"Will he not rather say to him, 'Prepare supper for me, and gird yourself and serve me, while I eat and drink; and afterward you shall eat and drink'? Does he thank the servant because he did what was commanded?"

Again, the question is obviously rhetorical. Of course, the master wouldn't thank his servant. Jesus then moves on to the point of the story: "So, you also, when you have done all that is commanded you, say, 'We are unworthy servants; we have only done what was our duty.'"

This passage bruises our happy face, have-a-nice-day, democratic sentimentality. The master looks arrogant, sitting there alone at the table while his tired and hungry servant feeds him dinner. Why couldn't he ask his servant to join him? At least he should have let him take a shower first.

But I wept when I heard this passage. Why should I be excused from taking care of a woman in my church who was in bad trouble? Because I was tired and wanted a day off? Because I hadn't eaten at a good restaurant in months?

Taking care of the people in my flock is nothing more than my duty. Should I get a medal every time I do what I'm supposed to do? Of course not. Jesus' disciples had plenty of trouble understanding what it meant to be a servant, but at least they quickly understood that a servant serves. Jesus is our master, and we are to do what He asks of us.

We've heard these words in church countless times and read them in our Bibles; there's really nothing new or mysterious about them. "Jesus is my Lord," we say, "and I am the Lord's servant." These words seem to pass so easily, glibly, from our lips. But I think we rarely understand what these words really mean.

Too often, being a servant in the church today means getting ahead, manipulating others, doing what we want to do most of the time. It means little more than dressing up some very worldly modes of behavior in "religious" language.

If you don't understand what it means to be a servant, or if you understand but fail to act that way, be consoled. You are in the best company.

If you don't understand what it means to be a servant, or if you do understand but fail to act that way, be consoled. You are in the best company. Jesus taught His apprentices, or disciples, how to serve by word and example during his three years of personal contact with them. Yet they were ordinary like you and me. They so thoroughly and so consistently failed to grasp what He meant that the spectacle is almost comical.

JESUS' MODEL OF LEADERSHIP

When Jesus was transfigured in glory before his very eyes and joined by Moses and Elijah, what was Peter's reaction? He wanted to build three huts for these spiritual icons so they would stick around (and presumably give Peter great authority). The apostles still didn't understand even after Jesus rose from the dead. "Will you now restore the kingdom to Israel?" They asked on the mountain. Jesus' reply was to return to His Father.

For three years, Jesus taught about the Kingdom of God, and for three years His apprentices understood Him to mean a worldly kingdom. They looked forward to throwing their weight around in this kingdom, and they probably thought about how they would reward their friends, settle old scores with their enemies, and set up their relatives in good jobs once the kingdom came.

We know for a fact that they jockeyed among themselves for good jobs. This rivalry broke into the open one day when the mother of James and John had the gall to ask Jesus if he could please let one of her boys sit at His right hand and the other at His left hand in the kingdom. The other disciples were indignant when they heard about it, but I imagine it was because the woman asked first, not because they understood what the kingdom was all about. I can imagine them saying to each other, "Did you hear what Jim and Johnny's mother did? Did you ever hear such "chutzpa"?

They all wanted to be important officials in the kingdom under Jesus, of course. Jesus used this occasion to patiently explain the difference between service in the Kingdom of God and worldly authority in the secular realm.

He began with the model of leadership they were most familiar with. "You know that the rulers of the Gentiles lord it over them," He said, "and their great men exercises authority over them."

Jesus' followers certainly knew this, since the Romans installed a puppet king over Israel, were shipping off the olive oil, figs, and wine of the land while taxing the people until they bled. They hampered their religious observances, of course. A crop of ambitious Jewish sycophants, flatterers, and fellow travelers had sprung up around the court of these pagans like mushrooms in a damp dark basement. Even the reformers—the Pharisees—were after power. They wanted to gain control of the religious life of the people.

> We replace all this with leadership as service. We are to help other people. Being nice. Doing what the Lord wants done. Serving.

Yes, the disciples knew all about rulers who "lord it over them." We know all about this too, don't we? In fact in our day, we do tyranny a lot more efficiently and ruthlessly than the Romans did. To this model, Jesus contrasts His own.

"It shall not be so among you," He said. "But whoever be great among you must be your servant, and whoever would be first among you would be your slave."

Jesus ends by offering Himself as the new model.

"Even as the Son of Man came not to be served, but to serve, and to give his life as a ransom for many."

This sounds attractive, doesn't it? We become Christians and make a clean break with all those ugly world-system authorities—the money-grubbing con men and women whom we have to do business with, the ambitious politicians, the unreasonable bosses we work for, the blood-thirsty tyrants who oppress most of the people in the world. We replace all this with leadership as service. We are to help other people. Being nice. Doing what the Lord wants done. Serving.

Sound easy? No, not really. It must be hard. Not many of us serve in the Jesus Way. I don't. In fact, I don't see many people in the churches that do. Most of us do fairly worldly jobs in church and call them "service" and adopt a worldly role and call it "servant." The radical transforming power of the Lord hasn't penetrated, and oftentimes we don't really want it to.

When the Lord began to radically change my way of pastoring back in the late 1970s, He started with my concept of being a servant. At the time I was perceived as an expert in church growth. I would fly all over the country telling ministers how to release growth in their churches. And I was good at what I did. People praised me, so I thought God must like it too. I was doing a lot for Him—as a servant of course. I was no brutal tyrant, and I didn't impose my will with a heavy hand. I didn't think I was a Sadducee or a Roman Governor. I diligently plucked the blossoms of Phariseeism that sprouted from time to time.

> Too often, being a servant in the church today means getting ahead, manipulating others, doing what we want to do most of the time.

Nevertheless, I was a man on the make. I was a success, and I measured success in the church the same way any red-blooded American did—by the numbers.

The Lord showed me how wrong this was. In obedience to

Him, I stopped doing the church growth seminars, went home, and waited for my next ministry trip to emerge. I waited. And waited. And waited, and finally told the Lord, "Time's a wasting here Lord. When do I start calling on people telling them about You?"

I heard the Lord say, "Come before Me, John."

"Lord," I said, "I'm an evangelical. Don't you know what an evangelical is? I'm called to be an evangelist. That's the highest need of the church."

"I heard the Lord then say, "Get rid of your office, and shut off your telephone." He then said, "Just worship Me. Cry a lot."

The Lord led me to the story of Martha and Mary. I'd always disliked this story; in fact, Mary was one of my least favorite people in the Bible.

"She's a wimp, Lord," I complained. "I don't like people who sit around and do nothing. I'm an activist, and I've got things to do and things to see."

"Am I among them?" I heard the Lord say.

"Well, sure you are, Lord, You're among them. I'm doing all this for You."

Then I was a bit shocked, feeling like I heard the Lord's response back to me.

"No, John, you're not doing it for Me, you're doing it for you. You want to be a success."

And that stung me. The word of God cut right down to the marrow that time. I could see that the Lord was right. I wanted to make it in this career I was in. I looked back on my life and began to understand what the Lord had done for me and where I stood in relation to Him.

He had saved me at the age of 29 when I was on the road to hell. The Lord threw me a lifeline and pulled me off that trolley. In the years since, my marriage got better; my kids got straightened out, my family prospered and other blessings showered down in great abundance. But none of that was promised to me the night I knelt on my best friend's living room floor and sobbed my guts out in thanksgiving. It was enough to be saved. I don't even think anyone mentioned heaven that night. They just told me I didn't have to carry my sin anymore. I was so glad to get rid of it.

How did this miracle come about? I realized I couldn't handle my life anymore, and I asked Jesus to become Lord of it.

And what did that mean?

It means that He was Lord and I wasn't. That was the whole point. I asked him to be Lord of my life because I had made such a mess of the job, and no longer wanted to do it, mostly because I knew I couldn't do it. I was a servant now, an underling. I am just a fellow who took instructions and relied on the master's power to see that the orders were carried out.

Sometimes when I stroll through a Christian bookstore or hear some preacher on TV, I wonder why everyone doesn't become a Christian. The Christianity package includes material prosperity, a better marriage, pious kids, better management, a better sex life, a budget that works, a self-image that will knock your socks off, and godly grooming and skin care. These benefits really are showered on Christians often enough. Why doesn't everyone line up to get theirs?

Maybe because all these benefits are beside the point. We are here to serve God's purposes, not our own. And the truth is some of us are blessed materially, and some of us aren't. Some have better marriages after their conversion, and some don't. But every Christian must make Jesus the Lord of his or her life. We've been saved from eternal death, not to follow our own fantasies, but do to God's will and serve His purposes.

It's hard to do this. Fortunately, the Lord has given us the ability to be faithful servants. God's Holy Spirit guides and empowers us, but it's also a fact that the very act of conversion to Christ frees us from the slavery to old models and passions.

I live in Southern California, and in that part of the country there is no more fitting time to have a dialogue with God and learn important spiritual truths while sitting in traffic on the freeway. That's the place where I learned about the status of my conversion to Christ. This dialogue occurred while I was struggling with the new ministry I wanted, but also which the Lord was keeping me from. As I was driving, God began to show me all the conversions I had experienced in my life. The first was my conversion to Pall Mall cigarettes when I was 13. There was a succession of others: to music, to several different styles of life, to groups of people, to an ideal of success, and to a certain pattern of relationships.

A common thread linked each conversion. I had done each out of desire to be successful. I wanted to be known and become someone. A terrible thought surfaced: Did I convert to Jesus Christ for the same reason? Because I thought maybe it would make me feel like I had become someone?

Then I heard the Lord speak to me.

"John, when are you going to believe that you are someone? I made you someone. I purchased you with My blood, and I've called you to be mine. Stop worrying about who you are."

I was so overcome with emotion that I pulled to the side of the road and opened my Bible. I opened to John's gospel, chapter two—the story of the Baptism of Jesus. My finger fell right on the words, "This is my Son, in whom I am well pleased." I was puzzled.

"I don't understand, Lord."

"That's the point John," I heard the Lord say. "You don't understand. How much service had I given my Father up to that point?

"None, Lord."

"That's right John, and already He was well pleased."

This instance was a reality check. I had already known the Lord for fourteen years and had always been looking for approval from Him. Now I realized that approval came as the Father saw His Son in me, not from the work I did. The key is the relationship. Jesus has relationship with the Father, and I have relationship with Jesus. The essence of these relationships is the same: master and servant. At last I was beginning to understand.

What does a servant do? The easy answer is to say that a servant serves, because he does what the master wants done. In our case, all creation is subject to our Master because He is a King with a realm so large that many things need to be done. We do the King's work.

And what is this work? There is a terribly inflated mystique about "service" in the church. "The Lord's work" tends to be solemnly intoned and relegated to the purview of religious specialist, becoming identified with highly visible "ministries" such as teaching, preaching, and church planting, or with being an elder, pastor, or counselor.

The truth is that the Lord's work is humble caring. Everybody should serve this way, and we should do so gladly. We learn how to be servants of the master by imitating the way our master serves the Lord. Jesus did the Father's bidding on earth; in fact His Father's will is all He did! He spent many hours in fellowship seeking His Father's will, living a life of total dependence on His Father's presence, voice, and directives.

One of the best portraits of Jesus the servant is found in Philippians. Here Paul describes the indescribable self-emptying of God becoming human:

> *Who, being in very nature God, did not consider equality with God something to be grasped, but made himself nothing, taking the very nature of a servant, being made in human likeness. And being found in appearance as a man, he humbled himself and became obedient to death—even death on a cross!*
>
> *– Philippians 2:6-8*

The word translated "servant" could also be translated "slave." Read the passage again with that word and think about it. Jesus came as a slave. It's bad enough to be a servant, but at least servants have some rights. Servants get paid. Servants can quit. Servants can file a grievance about working conditions with the shop steward of the servants union. But the slaves have no rights. They are owned by the master they serve.

When God became human, He came as a slave. Think about what this says of God's character.

God-the-human even led a slave's life, virtually devoid of the "blessings" the books say Christians should enjoy. Jesus was estranged from His family. He was celibate and had no family of His own. He had no education, no wealth or property, no status, not even a home. He spent the last three years of His life as a wanderer with no place to lay His head. He died a criminal's death. He lived and died this way in obedience to His Father's will.

Here is your model for your service as a servant.

And what does the service look like in our lives? Paul writes to the Christians, and explains how they were to relate and serve each other. "Complete my joy by being of the same mind, having the same love, being in full accord and of one mind," he writes.

Does this sound like your church? How about your Bible study group? It doesn't?

Well, Paul goes on to say, "Do nothing from selfishness or conceit, but in humility count others better than yourselves."

> A servant takes care of others first, then himself. The essence of servanthood is to live out your life for someone else.

The "humility" that Paul refers to here is not a groveling concession that everyone else is more gifted, more beautiful, and more worthwhile than you are. It refers to status. The servants in God's household treat everyone else as if they had a higher status in the kingdom. A servant takes care of others first, then himself. The essence of servanthood is to live out your life for someone else. That's the kind of life Jesus led, and that's the kind of life we are called to as believers.

This is what authentic ministry is—caring and loving others. What are the greatest attributes of a servant? Well, it's like the parable of the talents. This story seems to suggest that the master prizes resourcefulness and crafty dealing, but really what the master is praising is faithfulness.

The first two servants get praised, not for their investments but for their faithfulness in what they were entrusted with. Multiplying their master's property was no more than their job, but they were rewarded because they did their job. The best thing a servant can do is to be faithful. "It is required of stewards that they be found trustworthy," Paul writes to the rebellious and complaining Corinthians. Paul salutes the Ephesians Christians by calling them "faithful in Christ Jesus." When Barnabus, representing the elders in Jerusalem, paid the first official visit to the church in Antioch, he exhorted them all "to remain faithful to the Lord with steadfast purpose."

Servants get ahead because they are faithful. Timothy's reliability brought him to Paul's attention. Later, still young, he is head of a large and flourishing church in Ephesus. Paul is careful to tell Timothy to be respectful of the older men who are under his care.

How different things are in the world.

When was the last time someone got a big promotion in your company simply because he or she had faithfully done a good job? Of course people talk about how important it is to be dependable, reliable, and faithful, but the rewards usually go to those who are reliably aggressive, dependably glib with a line of talk, and faithfully adept at playing the game of company politics.

Dare I ask you what qualities get people ahead in your church?

The rules are different in the Kingdom of God for a very simple reason: There is nothing we can do for God. He is at work in the world and can use us for His work if we choose to adopt the attitude of a humble servant, by listening to the Holy Spirit and acting accordingly. But we are useless to God if we cling to our worldly models of leadership and success.

But that is exactly what we do. We see a talented executive, an energetic salesman, a charming teacher, a brilliant thinker, and we say, "If only that person were saved, then God could do a lot!" And that is so backwards! God doesn't need him, but rather, he needs God.

We say, "Wow, now that is a creative person. He is full of good ideas. If only he would get saved and bring those ideas into the Kingdom." But again, God doesn't need good ideas; God wants servants.

Look into your past to understand the Lord's power that came to rescue you. Look at the evil in your own heart this very moment to understand the greatness of God's love. There are no superstars in the Kingdom of God! No chief executive officers, no flashy creative directors, no up-and-coming musicians; there are only servants whose eyes are always fixed on Jesus Christ. He is the model servant, the servant of all servants.

Too often our service in the Kingdom is lip service. Our lips say, "Of course, I want to always be under God's immediate direction and control." Meanwhile, our minds say, "But if you really want to get something done, you've got to make it happen." And we do all these things "in the name of the Lord," of course, but often it's not in the Lord's name at all.

The brutal fact is that our flesh rebels against submission to God's authority and control. It hates being off the center stage. We are infinitely resourceful in devising a host of approaches and techniques that will allow us to appear to be doing one thing, while the truth is we are really doing another. We say, "Lord, Lord" with our lips, but our hearts are far from God's heart.

Paul was countering this worldly model of leadership when he wrote his letters to the church at Corinth. The Corinthians were thinking in terms of factions: Who was in Paul's party? Who was in Apollos' group? Who in Peter's camp? Who had the upper hand? Which party was really running the stewardship committee? Paul writes:

> *This is how one should regard us, as servants of Christ and stewards of the mysteries of God.*
>
> *– 1 Corinthians 4:1 (RSV)*

We also are stewards, and God's stewards conserve, preserve, and protect the Gospel. They don't redesign the mysteries of God, improve on them, or edit them. A faithful Christian steward becomes an instrument which God uses to proclaim the Gospel. This is precisely what Paul did when confronted by the competitive Corinthians whose hearts were wandering from their master. He preached the Gospel. Again, Paul explains:

So let no one boast of men. For all things are yours, whether Paul or Apollos or Cephas or the world or life or death or the present or the future, all are yours; and you are Christ's; and Christ is God's.

— 1 Corinthians 3:21-23 (RSV)

All things are ours. Forgiveness, salvation, eternal life. We belong to Christ. And we steward the mystery and offer it to those who are hurting. It is more creative than your best idea; it contains more wisdom than your deepest insight; it brings more healing than your most solicitous care.

Take your place as a servant. Attend to God's presence in the inner room of your heart, and do what He tells you to do. Be faithful in it and let God's divine power flow through you.

Two

The Way In is The Way On

"I'M JUST CHANGE IN GOD'S POCKET; HE CAN SPEND
ME HOW HE CHOOSES."

For a number of years before the Harrogate meetings, I had a growing desire to enter pastoral ministry. However, I didn't know if God was calling me or whether it was simply a matter of my own personal desires. I went to Harrogate, England to participate in the ministry teams and on the Monday night, I was actually complaining to a friend that I had literally prayed about whether God was calling me to pastoral ministry dozens and dozens of times, but I still had no clarity on the issue. My friend said, "Rich, why don't you ask the Lord for a sign?" I said, "Oh, I used to pray like that as a baby Christian, but I don't ask God for signs anymore." My friend responded, "Rich, every pastor in the world kicks poor Gideon around, but God didn't! God is more than willing to give you the guidance you are looking for."

I thought: That makes sense. *And so I said to God, "Lord, if you want me to leave my teaching job at Ohio State University and become a full-time pastor, I am more than willing to do it. Would you please speak to me in any way you see fit by Wednesday evening before I see Marlene?" On Tuesday I had no break through, nor was there any communication from the Lord all day on Wednesday.*

On Wednesday evening we met in a large hall in Harrogate. I will never forget the way John Wimber began the meeting. He said, "I was planning to teach on healing tonight, but I feel like the Lord wants me to speak about the pearl of great price." And then he said, "Some of you tonight are wondering about whether God is calling you into full-time ministry. You will know it's the Lord when there is no more time. When it is the last hour, you will know it's God." I literally gripped the side arms of my chair. I thought to myself: Lord is everyone here praying about going into full-time ministry? Are John's comments meant for me? *Through the course of the evening as John talked about his own life and calling, there were seven very specific statements aimed directly at my situa-*

tion. By the end of the evening I knew that God had answered my prayer for a sign. A few years later I had shared this story with John and told him how instrumental he was in my calling to pastoral ministry. John had then shared with me a very unusual experience going down the elevator right before he was to teach that night. He felt the Holy Spirit tell him in the elevator to change his teaching from healing to the teaching on the pearl of great price.

He told his wife, Carol, what he sensed from the Lord, but he also added, "But I can't do that. Everyone here is expecting a teaching on healing. What should I do?" Carol in her customary bluntness, said to John: "Well, John, if you are not going to do what the Lord tells you to do, why don't you quit Christian ministry all together?" John said, "Well, I can't do that." To which Carol responded, "Then do what God told you to do."

Rich Nathan is an author and the senior pastor of Vineyard Church of Columbus, Ohio. He also serves on the board for the Association of Vineyard Churches USA.

THE MUSIC MAN

At the time I got saved I had produced two albums—not singles, mind you—that were in the top ten for the U.S. I was being offered a lot of money in advance to do more albums. I had to say "No." I had to take all my stuff in my study and studio, put it in a truck and take it out to the dump. God wouldn't even let me sell it to anybody. He made it clear to me not to sell it. Without detailing how He did it, it is enough to know that when God wants all of you, He will make it clear what is standing in the way between you and Him. If you pay attention, you'll know what God is asking you to do.

During this time my wife and I went eight weeks without a paycheck. I was offered several opportunities, but the Lord said, "No!" These opportunities came while we were receiving groceries on our doorstep and living without air conditioning in the middle of a hot summer. I couldn't believe it! When I worked for the devil I made money. Now that I was working for God I was left with nothing, or at least that's what I thought at the time. About fifteen weeks after I had come to Christ, a nice man in the church came and offered me a terrible job. I joined a work force as an ordinary warehouse worker. I have almost no mechanical skills, yet I was hired into a manufacturing plant that builds things. I had never punched a time clock, worn those kinds of clothes or gotten dirty in any job I'd ever had. I didn't know what it felt like to do that; it was so foreign to me that I would be sick just going into the building each morning.

> **If you pay attention, you'll know what God is asking you to do.**

The thousands of hours I had invested in my fingers were being replaced with manual labor. I could play nineteen instruments professionally. Throughout the ordeal, I comforted myself in the back of my mind, thinking, God's just taking it away for awhile, He's a good God, He's probably going to give it back to me later. But it never happened. God didn't say, "If you give Me that, I'll give you this." He just said, "Obey me!"

That was over thirty years ago. God didn't call me into the ministry right away, either. That didn't come until much later, after I had given Him everything. But I have never regretted any of this because God's plan for my life far exceeded my own. I can honestly say that my life is His life working in me, not the fruit of my own effort or skill.

Jesus says, "I am the vine and you are the branches" (John 15:5). See, it's not my fruit, but Jesus' fruit. It isn't the fruit of my effort, my discipline, or my hard work; it's the fruit of His Spirit and work in me.

LOVE AND OBEDIENCE: THE BETTER LIFE

Jesus says, "Whoever has my commands and obeys them, he is the one who loves me. He who loves me will be loved by my Father, and I too will love him and show myself to him" (John 14:21). There's a direct correlation between your love for Jesus, the corresponding love of the Father, and your willingness to obey His commands. And by the way, one of the telltale signs that you are following the Lord passionately is that lukewarm Christians will find your zeal irritating!

In her book, *The Christian's Secret to a Happy Life*, Hannah Whitall Smith touched on this in her day, saying, "The standard of practical holy living has been so low among Christians that the least degree of real devotedness of life and walk is looked upon with surprise, and often with disapproval by a large portion of the church" (see chapter 15).

If you decide to go for life full-throttle as a Christian, you will meet with some disapproval, even in the community of saints because some members of the body are aggravated by this kind of passion. "Who do you think you are? Are you more spiritual than me?" Could it be that we are sometimes afraid that our own tepid condition will be revealed?

We must set our standards based on the injunctions of Scripture. That's what Hannah is urging. She says, "For the most part, the followers of the Lord Jesus Christ are satisfied with a life so conformed to the world in almost every respect that, to a casual observer, no difference is discernible" (see chapter 16).

It's sad but true that many Christians have so little of God functioning in their lives that no one will ever walk up to them and say, "What is it about you? Tell me, how did you take that situation so well?" We need to aspire to living a life that communicates the higher, better…the only life.

WALKING IN THE SPIRIT

Trusting, obeying, abiding, believing, studying, serving, loving, devoting, and consecrating; these are all action words to describe a committed Christian. Wouldn't it be great if we could live in the purity of these conducts and attitudes? What do we do about sin? When I fall short I want to know that I can return to that sense of God's pleasure over me.

That's what walking in the Spirit is all about. Becoming a Christian is the simple step of receiving the free gift of the finished work of Jesus Christ, repenting of our sins and then walking in this new revelation. Living out the Christian life requires a moment-by-moment relationship with the Lord.

Years ago I taught a series called, "The Way In is the Way On." Simply put, Christianity is a life of revelation in which you see

Christianity is a life of revelation in which you see yourself as limited and God as unlimited.

yourself as limited and God as unlimited. We have continual need of God's complete purity.

I came to Christ because I needed forgiveness and I continue in Christ needing forgiveness. The way in is the way on. When we develop a bad attitude or become self-righteous, we become something less than who we are in Christ. I understand the Christian way as the life of brokenness. It's a life in which we have to deal continually with sin and remember that He is righteous and therefore, we are righteous: "The eyes of the Lord are on the righteous and His ears are attentive to their cry" (Psalm 34:15).

THE SOVEREIGNTY OF GOD

Psalm 33:11 says, "The plans of the Lord stand firm forever, the purposes of his heart through all generations."

In response to trials and testing in our lives, we begin with the understanding that God is all-pervasive in the lives of people. This passage reveals that each of us has a place in God's kingdom.

Our Father has lovingly planned our lives. No event or circumstance takes God by surprise. He is on our side and makes the best choices for us. That doesn't mean that we won't go through difficulty. It simply means that we can trust and rely on God's decisions. Eventually, the end thereof will be our betterment, whatever it involves.

The Holy Spirit supplies us with peace when we yield our control over the events in our lives. The Lord responds to our cries, sometimes by granting transformation, rescue or healing. Other times He allows for time and pain to achieve some other end. The focus of our attention is not to be fixed on the pleasing or unpleasing results of our circumstances; our gaze should rest on God who is in control.

As Christians, we are called to have confidence in who God is and what He reveals in Scripture as adequate for life and godliness. We are called to obedience. This obedience is not accomplished through acts of service alone, but in giving ourselves in totality to Christ. Then we will yield fruit that remains from the best soil. For instance, a maid can do everything a wife and mother can do, but it is done from a different motivation. The maid serves for money, but a wife serves because she loves. Giving and service should never be divorced from one another, but one should flow from the other.

The results of our abiding haven't been tallied yet; however, they are being developed. The tabs are being taken daily. Certainly all of us at the end of the day have to call out for grace and mercy, don't we? But day by day, week by week, and year by year, God is making something beautiful out of you and me. He is producing in us the character, qualities and fruit of our Savior, the Lord Jesus Christ.

Keep your focus on Jesus. Concentrate on the realization that God is on your side and He is good. God loves you, and you are precious to Him. Your efforts to please Him on the one hand don't satisfy, but on the other hand, they always please. The Father won't rest until you are just like His Son, but He enjoys every little effort you make to try and be like Him. Keep it up, and remember: He is easy to please, but hard to satisfy.

> He enjoys every little effort you make to try and be like Him. Keep it up, and remember: He is easy to please, but hard to satisfy.

IF YOU LOVE ME

I want to give you three basic earmarks of this life of obedience found in the Scripture. We begin with the love for God and His commandments. It seems that it's not just enough to do what God says, but we must also love Him as well.

Jesus says in John 14:15, "If you love me, you will obey what I command." That's a simple statement, isn't it? If you love then you will obey. Obedience flows out of the depth of love we have for the Lord. You might ask, "How much obedience is enough?"

Then I'll ask you, "How much do you love your Lord?" How much reward do you want? How much peace or joy? Frankly, I can't get enough. I started out not needing much obedience or blessing, but as my love for Jesus grew, I became an addict. I have found that the older I get the more I have learned to deeply love the things of God. The more I see of God, the more I see the things of God worked out in life. I find that I want to be with Him even more. Consequently, I find myself becoming, by God's grace, a more obedient person as I prepare to spend eternity with Him.

Sometimes I wake up in the middle of the night full of joy, anticipating that moment when I get to be with my Lord, Savior, and Master Jesus Christ. I can't wait. And that's the way we're supposed to feel about it. This reality propels us toward a life of devotion to Christ, His cause, and His church as no other. That's what obedience to Christ looks like.

Are you willing to always say "yes" to Jesus?

Trust in God is profound to me and so fundamental to everything that I understand in the Christian life. It's the belief that God is good, gracious, charitable, and favors us. All the Father wants is for us to put our hand in His hand and let him guide us through life.

Sometimes we act like distrusting, rebellious children. We say, "No, no. You might make me do something I don't want to do. You might make me go somewhere I don't want to go. You might make me different than I want to be." I don't mean to be too harsh because I understand this problem, but the truth is that God is generous, caring, and gracious towards us. He is so worthy of our trust.

So many of us are going to have a surprise when we stand before God on our final day. We will have missed how good our Lord is, how kind, loving and gracious. We'll discover that He had wanted to give us so much here and now but we couldn't receive it because we had fearful expectations.

Once again, Hannah Whitall Smith's excellent book, *The Christian's Secret of a Happy Life*, brings something to bear here. Smith was talking with a physician who was having a lot of difficulty with doubts, unbelief, and fearfulness towards God. She said, "Well, doctor, if there were somebody here in the hospital that you could treat and was under your care, but they just simply couldn't trust you to take the medication, the direction, and treatment that you wanted to give, what would you do with that patient?" He said, "Well, I couldn't do anything with a patient that didn't trust me." And Hannah said, "Well, that's the way it is with you and your God."

Wow! Imagine what God could do in and through us if we just trusted Him, abandoning ourselves to Him in each moment.

People have said to me, "I can submit to things that come from God, but not to trials and testing that come from people. If God were doing those things, I would feel differently."

But God is allowing those things. You see, God is sovereign and over every circumstance of the believer's life. God is not the agent of trials, but He does often allow them in our lives. The truth is, nearly everything in life comes through human instrumentality. Most of our trials are the result of somebody's failure, ignorance, carelessness, or sin ... including our own.

If this is true though, where do we perceive the sovereign hand of God in it all? It is a mystery, but God works through everything in your life. God has chosen you, initiated a relationship with you, and taken you on as His "pet project", if you will. Because you are His, everything that comes toward you or seeks after you has the hand of God, the presence of God, and the will of God behind it.

I've been asked, "If somebody does something mean and dreadful to me, is that the will of God?" Not exactly. These actions are initiated by people (or the enemy), but by the time they get to you, they changed into the will of God. Otherwise they wouldn't have happened; God would have thwarted them in some way.

We need to avoid hasty either-or generalizations; God will not be tamed. I have often said, "If God is your friend, you don't need an enemy." God will allow things to come into your life that will cultivate fertile soil for the fruit of the Spirit to grow.

God gives us lots of opportunity to mature in Him, and much of the time these "growing pains" arrive through people. From a divine perspective, what happens *to* you is not as important as what happens *in* you.

But the fruit of the Spirit is love, joy, peace, patience, kindness, goodness, faithfulness, gentleness and self-control. Against such things there is no law.

– Galatians 5:22-23

PRACTICAL LIVING

It is important to undergird our faith with foundational understandings. Once we have some grasp of our justification before God by faith, the sanctifying work of the Holy Spirit and God's sovereignty in using whatever means He deems necessary for the work of the Kingdom, we are substantially rooted. We are ready to look at how we can walk out our faith in practice. There's a little chorus by J.H. Samuels and D.B. Towner that I learned in my early days as a Christian that carries the key message for Christians of all ages:

Trust and obedience are two sides of the same coin, yet they deserve individual attention.

"Trust and obey, for there is no other way to be happy in Jesus than to trust and obey."

These words sum up what is incumbent upon us in order to live a healthy Christian life. Trust and obedience are two sides of the same coin, yet they deserve individual attention.

Picture a mother at the beach with her toddler. His enthusiasm draws him like a magnet to the rolling waves that crash and spray on the shore. Instinctively his cautious mother hovers nearby and keeps a hand on her little guy to steady him while the water swirls around his ankles and knees.

As he gets older, the mother's position on the beach changes. Now she lets her boy wade a bit farther out while she keeps a watchful eye, ready to spring into action. By the time the boy reaches twelve, she is up at the beach, chatting with a friend while he surfs on his boogie board with only her visual supervision.

Trust is a natural process of maturation. We let go of the control of our lives little by little as time goes by. And the Lord is faithful to us; as our relationship unfolds, the trust becomes mutual.

How can we obey someone we don't trust? We can't and we don't. Trusting God is foundational to joyful obedience. Obedience is carried out after trusting Jesus implicitly.

We consecrate our wills to live for Christ no matter what the mitigating emotions or circumstances, which really is the first act of obedience for every Christian. And we joyfully serve Him, not out of some grim sense of duty or pride, but because of the love affair we can have with our Father through Jesus.

Sometimes we are tempted to wonder if we can obey in a complete enough way to become like Jesus. After all, we are as imperfect in our trusting of God as we are in other areas of life. When we look at ourselves, we think, *I'll never make it.*

But when we look at God and His Word, we know we will. It will not be by our doing but by our surrendering:

> *This is what the Sovereign Lord, the Holy One of Israel, says: In repentance and rest is your salvation, in quietness and trust is your strength, but you would have none of it.*
> *– Isaiah 30:15*

In essence, obedience can be defined as utter surrender to the one we trust. Take a potter, shaping moist clay on a spinning wheel: What does the clay have to do except stay put while the potter molds and makes it into the thing of beauty that he desires? We must stay pliable and yield to the Potter's hand.

The life characterized by faithful obedience is earmarked by fidelity to the revelation of God in Scripture and surrender worked out in the daily rhythm of Christian spiritual disciplines. In this way our wills are consecrated to carry out the concrete expressions of our faith regardless of our feelings, gifting, or circumstances.

Once when I was sharing about the surrendered life, a young man asked me, "Do you mean you always obey?" I said, "Oh no, I don't always obey. But whenever I don't, I'm sorry, and I repent and I go right back to obedience because that's what I believe we are called to do."

He replied, "Do you get better at it?" I felt I could honestly answer him, "Yes, I have." As I look back now over thirty years, there are a lot of things that I no longer have an appetite for and that don't tempt me as they used to. Many of my old desires are just gone.

I like what one of the great teachers of the past has expressed about the will. The 16th-century mystic and Archbishop Francois Fenelon has been a great blessing to the church down through the ages. When he talked about religion and our relationship with God, he said something to this effect, "Pure religion [our relationship to God] resides in the will, alone." In other words, though our emotions play a significant part in the relationship we have with God, acting out our faith depends on the exertion of our will. Obedience is something we do—inspired or uninspired—because we commit our wills to be in alignment with God's purposes and directives.

MOUNTAIN-STYLE OBEDIENCE

I think a life of obedience is about being supple, ready to serve, and willing to be corrected and molded as God chooses.

Paul wrote to the church gathering in Rome:

> *Therefore, I urge you, brothers, in view of God's mercy, to offer your bodies as living sacrifices, holy and pleasing to God—this is your spiritual act of worship.*
>
> *– Romans 12:1*

I call this "mountain-style" obedience, that is, lock, stock, and barrel surrender; no holds barred; everything given to God. Plunging your entire being into the depths of God. When I was presented with this gospel, I went for it. Not only did I bow my head, bend my knee, cry and pray the prayer, but I also gave myself. I did not "invite Christ into my life"—this is a different posture than the one I am advocating. I gave myself to Jesus. Do you see the difference? This is my understanding of the proposition. I was to abandon the pursuit of my personal life.

Paul encapsulated this when he gave us the evocative picture of offering our bodies as "living sacrifices." Worship isn't only singing songs and expressing heartfelt thanks and praise to a worthy God. Nor is it simply giving God your tithes and offerings.

Worship is the complete, wholehearted commitment of a being to another Being. You and me, unto Him. Whether you drive a truck or pull teeth for a living, you are all about Jesus! We will explore what it means to live worship as a whole-life expression in chapter six.

THE ART OF TRUSTING

Trust is letting go of our need to control outcomes, letting God be God. When I taught in this area with my congregation, the internal conflict of choosing to trust God came home to me when a member of our church shared her story with me:

Two years ago I came to the realization that aborting three of my children when I was young was a sin. I went to God and repented. Part of that repentance included the Compassionate Life Ministries program at the Anaheim Vineyard for women who have had abortions. It was there that I received healing and forgiveness from God. My husband and I then realized we really did want children. Up to that point I didn't want to have anything to do with them.

Last year we got pregnant twice, and we miscarried both of the babies. It was on October 3, 1995 that John Wimber told the congregation that he felt like the Lord wanted to heal barren women. When my husband and I went forward, the Lord asked me, "Do you trust me?" And I thought back, "I lost two babies this year, Lord. I did what you told me to do. I repented and received healing, and now you want me to trust You?"

"No, I don't trust You," I had to admit. "I can't go through any more death; I just can't do it." I was in agony. He whispered back to me, "If you don't trust Me, I can't bless you."

At that moment, I realized I was at a crossroads and had to make a decision. I was tying God's hands and He couldn't do anything until I trusted Him. Still, I had to be honest. "I don't trust you, God. I can't make that up. Help me. I want to trust You. I want to learn to walk with you." Two days later our doctor called and said that he had found out why we kept losing our babies. A month later, we conceived. Baby Faith was born nine months later and full of life.

She went on to share that from that point in time when she

decided to trust God with her life, that even in more challenging circumstances, she had learned the art of trusting. "He's so much better at my life than I am," she said.

SOVEREIGN AND LOVING

Trusting in God means believing in the absolute reliability of His character and Word. In the mid-90s when I returned to the pulpit after my year with cancer, I was amazed to discover that many in our congregation were not on the same page theologically or experientially.

As I described earlier, when I came to Christ and prayed the prayer of faith, I ended my life and began a new life in Christ.

Everything from that day until now has been Jesus. I like to say, "Just color me Jesus." It's not about my prior existence; in fact it's not even about adding a little religion to my life. It's about ending one phase of life in a very real sense. I cut off all considerations of my identity and past, and gave myself totally over to Jesus Christ in every way that I knew how. I died in 1963.

Trusting God is pivotal to this whole business of being a Christian. Without this understanding, I could not have faced

> Trusting God is pivotal to this whole business of being a Christian. Without this understanding, I could not have faced heart attacks, cancer, treachery, and violence—people threatening me with guns and bombs.

heart attacks, cancer, treachery, and violence—people threatening me with guns and bombs. These are just some of the things that have gone on in my life. These externals are on one side; on the other side lay my own frailty, failures, and weaknesses as a human being. Sometime these are more frightening than anything else I face on a daily basis.

What about you? Have you signed over your life to God? Is He entrusted with the processes and outcomes of your life? This is not primarily a theological discussion, but an active decision and habit of the heart. We must come to God knowing that He is who He claims to be: sovereign and loving.

Three

Remembering the Poor

"WE NEED THE POOR AS MUCH AS
THEY NEED US."

Ever since I met John in 1982 I knew that the poor and the lost were a priority in his heart and in his life. I heard this through stories that he recounted about taking people into his own home.

The very last time I was with him was at a conference in Canada on "Justice and Ministry with the Poor." I was so excited to be at such a conference with the opportunity to hear John speak; I wondered why he had ever done any other conference, as this was so much a part of his being. He recounted stories about his children and his grandchildren and how helping the poor and giving to the poor was a normal and exciting part of their own walk with Jesus. In fact, it was so much a part of his family's experience that it seemed he wondered why it would not be a part of anyone else's.

Ministry with the poor has always been one of the Vineyard's stated values, and I have longed to see this properly worked out all over the world. I thank John for his own example.

Jackie Pullinger-To oversees the St. Stephens Society, a rehabilitation center among the poor in Hong Kong.

———◆———

Shortly before the Vineyard started (while John was with Fuller Evangelistic Association), he called me one evening from Tennessee where he was teaching at a church convention. This was a gathering of a denomination that had been started, as John put it, with fire from heaven that fell on the poor farmers and uneducated masses in the area. John called me weeping, after being with these folks for a few days. He had been up all night reading and praying over Isaiah 58.

"If you spend yourself on behalf of the hungry, and satisfy the needs of the oppressed…" He described their old evangelist with his voice blown out from the years of preaching out in the fields. "There wasn't a sound in that enormous tent except the rough, broken

voice of that old man calling the people back to God and to the ministry they were called to by God. He told them to get rid of their shiny new cars and leave their big houses and throw away their fancy clothes. 'Go find your old overalls and work boots and go out to the needy again,' he said. 'Feed them like you used to ... help 'em like you did before when you'd clean their babies for them and heal their sick little ones. That's how you started! Go back where you started! Go back where you began! Go back to God!'"

John listened and watched as the conviction of the Holy Spirit rested on these people and the weight of God's presence moved them like wind over a field of wheat. The only sound was a deep, quiet moaning. With every continuing word spoken, they swayed one way, and then the other.

John told me it was the most powerful time he had ever experienced. And I can verify that he did experience it! I wept with him. "The weight of God bent me with them," he told me. "I can't quit crying." Then he said (and to feel the full impact of this, you have to know that John had been adamant about being through with pastoring), "Carol, if the Lord ever calls me to pastor again (still sobbing), I want us to minister to the poor, the hungry and the needy, OK?"

"OK," I said, and apparently God said OK, too.

Carol Wimber was married to John for 42 years until his passing in 1997.

———◆———

Our responsibility to the poor was etched into our spirits right from the beginning as the Lord made it a personal issue with us in the Vineyard. It is something the Father entrusted to us and something we must guard and cherish because it is very, very important to Him.

One evening there was a meeting at our house, when the church was just beginning, and the power of God was being poured out on us and we didn't know what it all meant. To be honest, we didn't know what to do with this power. So we asked Juan Carlos Ortiz, who had been brought by a friend, if he had some wisdom for us. We knew (or at least we thought) that he was a Pentecostal and therefore had already been around this block a few times.

He took us aside and looked at us soberly for a long time, as if to determine whether we seriously wanted advice or not. Finally he spoke:

> The Pentecostals have always had wonderful celebrations and glorious meetings. We have spent the power on our glorious meetings and celebrations. My advice to you is to use the outpouring of the Spirit in doing good for the poor. Spend the power of God on helping the poor.

This wisdom really hit Carol and I both. And from the beginning we felt this reality. If we ever ignore the poor and needy, we're as good as dead as a people. We have our instructions. (And you know what? We've found that when we take care of the poor, we have some mighty fine celebrations, too!)

> **If we ever ignore the poor and needy, we're as good as dead as a people.**

Shortly after this encounter, Monty and Brandy Whitaker came to me and shared their heart for the poor. They had already shared everything else they had with the poor. They had emptied their cupboards and closets for those in a park nearby.

"Isn't it the duty of the church to take care of the poor and those in need?" they asked.

I listened and I could see their passion come alive. I could not help but reply, "You are the church, Monty and Brady; keep doing it!"

They did keep on doing it and the obvious anointing of God was on them. So, I asked them to come and train the church in the ministry that was already taking place daily in their lives. Sure enough they did, and sure enough it flourished and grew more and more throughout the years.

Carol and I believe that *the main reason God's hand has stayed on the Vineyard is because of our commitment to the poor and needy.* Serving the poor just isn't an option for us. It is a life or death matter, and we have no choice here. Many American evangelicals do not realize this. This wasn't something Carol and I—or Monty and Brandy—thought up. This was entrusted to us. It is Jesus' ministry. He gave it to us and we will give an account to Him one day. His call to us is very clear and we'd best not ignore it! Jesus said:

If I had not come and spoken to them, they would not be guilty of sin. Now, however, they have no excuse for their sin.
– John 15:22

Also, the command Jesus has given us is simple and uncomplicated. Feed the poor. Clothe the naked. Heal the sick. Cast out demons. We don't need to find the "worthy" poor. How judgmental! We do not have the responsibility of determining who is worthy and who is not. We are not the ones to determine worthiness, only need.

Give generously to him and do so without a grudging heart; then because of this the Lord your God will bless you in all your work and in everything you put your hand to. There will always be poor people in the land. Therefore I command you to be openhanded toward your brother and toward the poor and needy in your land.
– Deuteronomy 15:11-12

Look at King Nebuchadnezzar—this guy ate grass for seven years! Is it luck that determines where or in what time, what family, what culture we are born into? Or is it the plan of the almighty God that we be His hands and feet in this place, in this time, in this culture with whatever resources He chooses to give us? The poor could be "them" one day, and "us" the next.

> We are not the ones to determine worthiness, only need.

Thank God Jesus calls the poor "blessed." Perhaps we should befriend the poor and see this blessing for ourselves.

We need to the poor.

We need the poor to work out our own salvation, and the poor need us. A prophet said our name in the Vineyard is *worship* and *compassion*. I hope that is true. We do love the worship that the Lord has given us. We cherish God's presence that accompanies the worship when His power to heal is right there with us.

The manifest presence and the power of the Holy Spirit in our midst is connected, inseparably, to His mercy and compassion.

God will not be treated like a smorgasbord as though we can pick and choose what suits us best. That's not the way that it works, it is impossible to have one without the other. We just wouldn't survive the surgery.

> *He upholds the cause of the oppressed and gives food to the hungry. The Lord sets prisoners free, the Lord gives sight to the blind, the Lord lifts up those who are bowed down, and the Lord loves the righteous. The Lord watches over the alien and sustains the fatherless and the widow.*
>
> *– Psalm 146:7-9*

The same Lord who gives sight to the blind and creates miracles through our hands is the very One who feeds the hungry through our hands, and who watches over the immigrant. We must never ignore the poor and the needy. We must never spend the outpouring of the Spirit on ourselves.

It is my opinion that the best way to become whole is to help others. I think there is a direct path to healing in ministering to the poor and needy. Unless this ministry is a major force in the church, we will become introspective and self-focused.

We get well in helping others get well.

PROTECTOR OF THE POOR

He will defend the afflicted among the people and save the children of the needy; he will crush the oppressor.

– Psalm 72:4

In the Old Testament there are several words concerning the poor that share the same Hebrew root meaning. In English, they are translated: weak, helpless, impoverished, oppressed, and needy. In God's eyes, these various aspects of poverty illustrate what it feels like to be poor. I've found around 30 verses alone in which the Lord tells us that He will be the protector of the poor. He has set Himself as judge over the affairs of men—particularly to rescue them from oppression.

He watches over employers who oftentimes line their own pockets and fail to pay their works a just wage. He notices the slumlords that demand exorbitant rents from their tenants. He sees those who sell substandard goods, which look like bargains but will fall apart in no time. The poor can appeal to men. They can cry out to their neighbors and friends and to the political mechanisms that are available; but they can also go over the heads of these people and present their case directly to God.

Because of the oppression of the weak and the groaning of the needy, I will now arise, says the Lord. I will protect them from those who malign them.

– Psalm 12:5

We must see our responsibility to relieve the poor and to enhance their circumstances. Not only must we feed and clothe them, we must also help them get good jobs so they can participate in our economy. The principle is always the same: You give someone a fish, teach him to fish for himself and finally give him a license so he can fish wherever he'd like. Many churches have gotten as far as phase one, but we must progress beyond that. The poor don't just cry out for immediate relief; they want to be integrated into society just like everyone else.

> The church is not an organization, but a company of people who lay down their lives for others.

We must keep in focus that God's heart is broken over the poor, the helpless, and the oppressed. If your timetable doesn't allow any time, you must reconsider your calendar. How do we defend the cause of the weak and the fatherless? You don't work through a structure so much as through a living body. The church is not an organization, but a company of people who lay down their lives for others. And as we catch God's heart and understand His compassion, He will lead us in ministry to the poor. This is a work for the Church, as individuals are shown the need by the Holy Spirit; not a time to step back and point your finger at the *organization* for not doing what you see is needed. All too often Christians who have a social consciousness accuse the Church for not meeting the needs of the poor when God is actually giving them His heart and sight so they would take up His leading in their life for this ministry.

Today, God looks for individuals who listen to His Word and respond to it. "Remember, the poor," He says. "Preach to them; lead them to Jesus; cast out their demons; minister to their physical and emotional need; help them to find employment and show them the way through the bureaucratic maze in your nation."

Wouldn't you love to hear His "well done—whatever you did for them, you did for Me"?

When John's disciples asked Jesus, "Are you the one who was to come?", the Lord not only pointed them to His miracles as proof of His Messiahship, but also to the fact that the good news is preached to the poor (see Luke 7:22b). The proclamation of the Gospel to the poor was one of the signs of the presence of the Kingdom.

> If we say to someone, "Go, I wish you well; keep warm and be well fed" but do nothing at all about his physical needs, we're preaching an incomplete Gospel.

Not only did Jesus bring the Word of God, he also performed the works of God. He taught the message of the Kingdom in what He said and what He did. If we say to someone, "Go, I wish you well; keep warm and be well fed" (see James 2:16b) but do nothing at all about his physical needs, we're preaching an incomplete Gospel. Jesus wants to relieve suffering, heal, deliver, as well as save. We must bring the mercy of God to bear on all the circumstances of life.

"Blessed are you who are poor," Jesus said, "for yours is the kingdom of God" (Luke 6:20b). It is a glorious promise. If the poor receive the message of salvation, they can enjoy the Kingdom both now and in eternity.

The Council at Jerusalem was convened to discuss a contentious issue: Should Gentile Christians "be circumcised and required to obey the Law of Moses" (Acts 15:5b)? After some discussion, they decided that the answer was no, but they did agree that the Gentiles should abstain from certain foods and sexual immorality. They then sent Paul and Barnabus along with Judas and Silas to the Gentile Christians with a letter containing the conclusions drawn by this Council. Acts 15:31 says, "The people read it and were for glad for its encouraging message."

When Paul wrote to the Galatians, he referred to this discussion, but added something, which was not recorded in Acts 15. In Galatians 2:10, Paul says, "All they asked was that we should continue to remember the poor, the very thing I was eager to do."

Likewise, God has time and time again encouraged the Vineyard to "remember the poor." On occasions, we've given thousands of dollars to disaster victims and collected great quantities of food and clothing to be sent to places that were in need. Several years ago, when God began pouring his Spirit in the Vineyard meetings, God spoke to me about how that was to translate into good works for our local community. This was an echo of what was spoken to Carol and me by Juan Carlos Ortiz in the very beginning stages of the Vineyard.

What happened was amazing. We then spent the next eighteen months refurbishing homes, sometimes virtually rebuilding about a hundred properties—putting in new floors, putting in new plumbing, putting on new roofs, along with new fences and gates. The believers were so thrilled about the outpouring of the Holy Spirit that they were anxious to pour out this newfound intimacy and power into an expression of love to the community.

CATCHING GOD'S HEART

God presides in the great assembly; he gives judgment among the "gods": "How long will you defend the unjust and show partiality to the wicked? Defend the cause of the weak and the fatherless; maintain the rights of the poor and

the oppressed. Rescue the weak and needy; deliver them from
the hand of the wicked."

– Psalm 82:1-4

Asaph prays with God's heart as he cries out for the "weak and fatherless," the "poor and oppressed." We will never step out of our middle-class mindset and do anything for the poor until we've caught God's heart for them.

> **We will never step out of our middle-class mindset and do anything for the poor until we've caught God's heart for them.**

Jesus exhorted His disciples to have a secret history before God. "When you give, pray and fast, don't let anyone know about it," He said. "If you do your acts of righteousness before men, the world may praise you, but there will be your reward." The more famous of them might decide to phone up the newspapers, and get their photos taken and give fabulous sums of money to some charity somewhere; finding the next morning their names and picture blazed across the press for all to see. Those who aren't quite as wealthy still seek recognition from others, but they do it in a more subtle way—maybe letting something slip out concerning the good they've done.

Christians aren't exempt from the desire to be noticed by others. Secretly we often want people to know how prayerful and generous we are. We find it difficult to maintain a simple life of simple devotion before God. When we announce our acts of righteousness to others we demonstrate that we want our reward from God in the here and now. If that's what you're after, that's what God will give you. But don't you think you would be more fulfilled if you set your sights on an eternal reward and lived for that instead?

I remember when I had been a Christian for about a year and clearly desiring to do something for the needy and praying for direction about it. At the time I could have been thought of as poor. Carol and I had four small babies, all under age six, and I had been out of work for several months. I did have a job at the time, but I was only bringing home $87 a week, and I was already tithing on that.

As I prayed, God showed me a picture of a hand, which was closed at first, but then it opened up. He then seemed to say, "The world tells you to have a tight-fisted hand, particularly if you are in need yourself. It says you've got to cling to everything you've got. It advocates a logical and sensible economy; but that economy is not Mine. I want you to see that everything is in My control and to live your life with an open hand. If you do that, I will give you ample resources both for yourself and for others."

We are called to give to the needy, but to do it in secret (see Matthew 6:1-4). We're not to bring attention to the good works or to ourselves. And the truth is too many people serving others are doing it for earthly acclaim.

The Israelite knew that in the seventh year the law required them to cancel all debts, so if you were an Israelite and if someone asked you for a loan in the sixth year, you might think, "I'm only going to get a tiny portion of this back, so I'm not going to lend him anything. Let him approach me in 12 months time." This attitude may seem justified in the world's economy, but it is sinful in God's eyes. If the needy person cries out against you, the Lord will hear him and hold you accountable.

God is a generous God. He gives in abundance and in profusion. Examine the Garden of Eden with its abundance, the book of Psalms and Proverbs with God's heart expressed in His desire to teach His people, the Prophets with their timely words exhorting Israel to forsake injustice and worship God by giving to the poor. And as you begin to explore the New Testament, Jesus teaches and acts continually on behalf of the poor.

God's way is always to encourage you to give and then to load you with blessing. I've seen it happen both in my own life and in the lives of others. I've seen people open up their hearts and homes, giving as generously as they possibly can, and God has always caught up with them. He has met their needs and lavished His riches on them.

Our motivation to give shouldn't stem from the desire to receive. We should simply want to obey God's command regardless of whether He rewards us or not. But the fact remains that if we open our hands to the needy, He will bless us in all our work and in everything we put our hand to. When we are generous with our time, our money and our energy; we are then reflecting His personality.

Often when middle-class folks come to our church and I start talking about "needing the poor," I can see people looking at their spouses, saying, "What do I need the poor for?" I tell them that, for one thing, giving a part of your life, some portion of your time and resources to people who are socially marginalized is central to your growth. I say, "You may have come to this church with all kinds of problems—you may be an angry person, or have alcohol problems, or you may just be a materialistic consumer, focused on getting ahead. Whatever it is you're struggling with, if you care for and serve the poor, you will find some of your own healing in the process."

Often folks will come up afterwards and ask, "Is that what this church does, serve the poor?" I say, "Yes." They say, "Well, do you have to do that to go to church here?" I tell them, "No, you don't have to—but it's your privilege ... and it may become your passion if you start doing it." Not everybody does, but most people in our church do. People come to me—some of whom have been Christians for twenty or thirty years—and they have never crossed that threshold. They never went out into a neighborhood, never stood in a dangerous place and sucked it up and said "Oh God, oh God" and knocked on a door and gave somebody some food. Later, they would often come back with tears in their eyes and say, "Thank you for insisting that we go."

JUSTICE FOR THE OPPRESSED

I love to teach on social justice! It really is one of my passions. Justice always goes hand in hand with true revival and renewal of the Spirit. Justice—setting things right for the poor and the marginalized—is one of the primary purposes for God sending His Son into the world. He came in order to set things right. Great leaders in the history of the church have always understood the relationship between faith and justice. There has never been a movement of God started on fire that did not have a ministry to the poor.

Here are some church leaders throughout history who were passionate about serving the poor [Drawn from the following illustrations from George Grant's Bringing in the Sheaves, revised and expanded. (Brentwood, TN: Wolgemuth & Hyatt, 1988, pp. 55-6 and 200-1)]:

Basil of Caesarea (330-379) established orphanages, schools, poorhouses, and hotels for poor travelers, caring for the thousands of poor and neglected that came to his city. He is best known for developing the first fully staffed hospitals.

He said,

> A man who has two coats or two pairs of shoes when his neighbor has none has his neighbor's coat and shoes. It evidences a lack of grace in his life. The redistribution of wealth is in no wise to the point. The revealing faith is the point.

John Chrysostom (347-407) was called the "golden-mouthed orator," for he is considered one of the greatest preachers in the history of the church. Yet he devoted more time and energy to service to the poor than to preaching! He established many Christian charities, hospices, and hospitals for the destitute.

He said,

> The essence of the Gospel is not concern for the poor but it certainly provokes that concern. In fact, without that concern, the essence of the Gospel surely has not been grasped.

Augustine of Hippo in North Africa (354-430) is probably the greatest theologian in the history of the church. Yet he also had a profound impact on the economy of North Africa through the development of works of charity in thirteen cities.

Gregory the Great (540-604) coordinated efforts to help victims of war, pestilence, and famine throughout his ministry. He both gave from his personal income and provided large amounts of money from the church.

Bernard of Clairvaux (1090-1153) is best known as the father of one of the greatest monastic movements in church history, which resulted in many people coming to Christ. He also established a network of hostels, hospices, and hospitals, which have survived to present day.

John Wycliffe (1329-1384) is best known for his English translation of the New Testament, which helped revive interest in the Bible and lead to the Reformation. He also led a grass-roots movement of lay preachers and relief workers who ministered to the poor.

Jan Hus (1374-1415) was a dynamic preacher, evangelist, and reformer who helped pave the way for Luther. He also organized an army of workers for emergency relief when Central Europe was struggling under war, famine, poverty, and moral degradation. He won the hearts of the people both through his preaching and good works.

He said,

> Doubt must be cast on fruitless lives. Profession must be

followed by deeds of charity, otherwise that profession is false.

Dwight L. Moody (1837-1899) is best known today as one of the greatest evangelists in the history of North America. He also established more than 150 street missions, soup kitchens, clinics, schools, and rescue outreaches.

Just look at how it works. Seeking justice and being moved by true social concern aren't options—they are marks of a true apprentice of Jesus. Still, how do we go about seeking social justice for the oppressed? The dilemma we face is rather simple really: If we are not to establish a theocracy or Christian state on earth, a "political" kingdom of God, then how are we to work for social justice?

Some evangelicals believe that God's Kingdom hasn't even arrived yet. This point of view stems largely from a relatively recent belief system known as

> I believe our focus should be on changing the church so she is conformed to God's justice and holiness.

"Dispensationalism," which has influenced many (though by no means all) American evangelicals. This view of the Kingdom of God traces its heritage from the Scofield Study Bible, which taught that we're living in a "church age" that is wholly separate from God's active reign on earth. They believe that God's Kingdom will be established on earth in some future millennium. They conclude from their view of the kingdom that all attempts to establish justice in this age are like "polishing brass on a sinking ship." The only legitimate and worthwhile activity for them is evangelism, which for them is the saving of souls for the afterlife.

There is a growing tendency among another subset of evangelicals to attempt to enforce a heavenly kingdom through an external "Christianizing" of society. They want to do this by enforcing

Old Testament laws in political and governmental practices today. They conclude that this new society under "God's law" will pave the way or usher in the Kingdom.

Neither of these approaches seem satisfactory to me. I believe that Jesus has shown us a third way that recognizes the first-fruits' presence of the Kingdom, here and now, but at work in a way that involves both individuals and communities, transcending politics-as-usual. I believe our focus should be on changing the church so she is conformed to God's justice and holiness. In this regard, the church acts as a counter-culture and social conscience, "salt" and "leaven" in the world-at-large. Our mission is the work of redemption in the world today, and including the salvaging of souls and caring for the physical and social needs of those we have contact with.

> I believe that loyalty to Christ means loyalty to His mission, His methodology, and His theology.

Furthermore, as soldiers, we would have to break rank in order to heed these competing voices. We have already been called to war; the Lamb's nonviolent war of restoration through the Gospel. The battle plan of this war is the preaching of the Gospel, healing the sick, feeding the hungry, nurturing the church, looking after the lost, the widow, and the bereaved. It is important that we do not leave our post in order to retreat to a privatized sphere of piety or to fight an alternative war on the world-system's political terms. We must remain steadfast to Jesus.

God has called us to be another way; to another form of battle. Scripture is clear that our war is not of this world and that the weapons of our warfare are of a spiritual nature.

We will not be effective at calling the world to peace and justice until we are purified and prepared. Our societies need us as salt and light.

So when we see problems of injustice and oppression in the world and turn to the world for methods and solutions to those problems, we run the risk of taking on their values and priorities. This is a problem of too many Christians today. I believe that loyalty to Christ means loyalty to His mission, His methodology, and His theology.

We must keep in mind that when our efforts to overcome injustice become detached from the work of spiritual transformation, we are on the road to being taken over by one of the agendas of the world-system. Only spiritual transformation gets to the root of injustice and oppression.

If you have passion in you to strike a blow against the injustice of abortion, win an abortionist to the Lord. If you're against drug abuse, win a drug dealer to Christ. If you don't like crooked politics, win a politician to the Lord. Then as these people are discipled and come under the Kingdom of God, they will be "salt and light" in the world, testifying to the Gospel. They will have a biblical philosophy they can take back to deal with the problems of abortion, drugs, or deceitful politics. In some instances they will even challenge and change evil social structures (Ephesians 6:12). They may even help change laws that condone abortion, alter social conditions that foster drug abuse, and transform governments that oppress the poor and deny basic civil rights.

Ask the Lord to fill you with His passion for those who are helpless to help themselves; ask Him for opportunities to serve others in your local community. I guarantee that Jesus will send you people to love on behalf of Him. What an awesome opportunity we have to be the hands and the feet of Jesus. We must never forget the poor and the oppressed among us. For when we give ourselves to others, our own healing will be waiting.

Four

Everything is Grace

"OH, GOD! OH, GOD!"

John was many things to me: precise and powerful, a father who used his power to bring out the best in me and countless others.

It was no small transition to watch this powerful man diminish physically. I had the privilege of knowing John best in the last year or two of his life. His frame was weak, his gait halting, and he did not hear well. He often looked otherworldly, as if waiting for release. Yet he was also at peace; he would light up when engaged in conversation and would share a meaningful word or two.

One Sunday night at the Vineyard Anaheim, he slowly climbed the steps to the lectern and gave a brilliant talk on ministry to the poor. Though a shadow of his normally robust self, I glimpsed a power far greater radiating through him. I witnessed a true power encounter that night—God mighty in poor vessels, extending His riches through them to feed many. Though weak, John was never more powerful to me than he was that night. I left filled and yet eager to give away what I had, more grateful than before for this man who allowed God to manifest through him until the end. May I honor him by doing the same all the days of my life.

Andy Comiskey is the founder of Desert Streams Ministries, a place of sexual and relational healing.

———◆———

S t. Theresa of Lisieux says, simply, that "everything is grace." Suffering is something, therefore suffering, too, is grace. This is what Paul implies in Romans 8:28 when he writes, "All things work together for good to those who love God." This is the most amazing verse in Scripture.

The difference this makes in everything, including suffering, is total. The alternative is Ecclesiastes' "vanity of vanities." Either our lives are pockets of darkness surrounded by ultimate light or pockets of light surrounded by ultimate darkness. How could we live if we believed the second?

We cannot know what God's purpose is in each event and every detail. But we can know that every event, each detail, is part of God's purpose. Everything is grace. Job's sores were grace. Job's abandonment was grace. Jesus' abandonment at the cross ("My God, My God, why have you forsaken me?") was grace. Our abandonment is also grace.

Our attitude toward God's involvement in every detail should not be one of passive resignation in life because our activity is a vital part of this divine grace, plan, and purpose. Our active struggle against suffering and every form of evil—physical, psychological, and spiritual—is part of God's will for us and part of our growth and learning. But at the same time as we say *no* to suffering, death, disease, and diminishment, we also say *yes* to God's hand behind it, allowing it. We affirm God's wise and loving plan that includes in its plot both our sufferings and our efforts to conquer them.

It is like being in a play; even as you are portraying the will of the character you are playing, you are also enacting the will of the author. We can be abandoned to God's perfect will for us even as we are actively struggling against every kind of evil.

OUR POOR PERFORMANCE

When I came to Jesus, I was tired of being what I was. I did not like who I had become. I ached to be good and virtuous, but I could never seem to get there. Finally, in despair, I reached out to Jesus as the response to this problem in my life. I understood that He had forgiven my past and present sins; it was the sins I would commit in the future that I was confused about.

I recall my wife Carol talking with me about this subject when we were new believers. Following our conversation she wrote a letter in which she said, "As a result of my understanding of the Word of God, I declare that I will not sin again." She signed it, dated it and hung it on our bedroom wall! It actually stayed there for years. But one day I came home and found it crumbled on the floor; I did not have to ask for an explanation. I thought that the Christian life was comprised of spiritual performance, similar to performance in the secular world. As a musician, if I did not perform well, I didn't have a job. I was accepted or rejected based on the quality of my performance.

I would try my best to perform pleasingly to God. I sometimes went for minutes without sinning! Every time I decided to pray, I was reminded how poorly I was doing and how it was no use to continue because God did not accept me. It was years before I understood that performance and acceptance were not tied to each other. God accepted me on the basis of what Jesus had done for me. All my "good" performance could not please God anyway.

Even today as I begin to pray, from time to time the forces of the enemy will play my poor performance before me on a giant screen. But over the years my heart has caught up with my head. I remind myself of what God has done for me in Jesus. Remember to remind yourself—it works!

John tries to describe in human language the indescribable glory of the Word made flesh:

> *The Word became flesh and made His dwelling among us. We have seen His glory, the glory of the One, and Only, who came from the Father, full of grace and truth.*
>
> *— John 1:14*

He uses two powerful words to capture the essence of the incarnate Word: grace and truth. It is the incarnate Word—Jesus—who is full of grace and truth. In his commentary on John, Leon Morris points out that the word *grace* in John 1:14 denotes "that which causes joy," and "winsomeness." It speaks of God's "good will" and "kindness" toward humankind. Though it is undeserved, God speaks gratuitous favor through Jesus Christ.

For the Christian, the highest expression of grace is God's provision for our spiritual need by sending His Son to be humanity's savior. God also speaks of the good gifts He imparts to those He saves. Finally, grace reminds us of the attitude of thankfulness we ought to have to God for all His goodness to us.

A MERCIFUL JUDGE

A few years ago I went to court with my youngest son. He had chosen to disobey instructions he had received from the court and as a result was about to face a judge for sentencing. Even today I don't fully know my son's rationale for not doing what he was told to do by the court to begin with, but he didn't. That morning, a court clerk told me that my son was about to be seen by one of the harshest judges in that court. This was not good news. I knew that my son was guilty of the charge. He realized and admitted it.

This knowledge did not make me pray for justice. In fact, I've noticed that when you're guilty of a charge, you don't want justice; you want mercy. I had prayed through much of the night before on the living room floor, sobbing and saying, "Oh God, have mercy on my son! I don't want him to go to prison."

That day while Carol, his fiancee, Christy, Sean and I were waiting, the clerk came to us and said, "You're not going to appear before this judge. You're going to appear before another judge." To our amazement, we left the courtroom of the harsh judge and appeared before another judge whose own teenage son had died the year before in similar circumstances.

This new judge heard the case that was presented, waited, and asked for the witness. He then weighed the whole thing and looked down at my boy and said words that still grip me when I think of them, "Son, you're guilty, but the court forgives you."

> I've noticed that when you're guilty of a charge, you don't want justice; you want mercy.

My son stood motionless. It didn't connect. I didn't get it either. Then the man smiled a beautiful, kindly, loving smile. He said, "You don't understand, son. There is no charge against you. Your case is dismissed. You can go." My son turned to look at me, and we both began to sob. The realization that his sin had been absolved was overpowering. I suddenly saw that the judge has the right to forgive. In that moment, I was reminded that the judge of heaven and earth has chosen to absolve me from my sin. We are guilty, but God has chosen to forgive. "It does not, therefore, depend on man's desire or effort, but on God's mercy" (Romans 9:16).

TO LIVE IS CHRIST

The ultimate goal of existence is to fellowship with Jesus forever. It is His prerogative to determine the course of our lives on our way to everlasting life with Him. We come to understand this at the foot of the cross. Before Jesus intersected our lives, we were pitiful sinners condemned to eternal alienation from God.

Paul writes in his letter to the church in Philippi, "Yes, I will continue to rejoice for I know that through your prayers and the help given by the Spirit of Jesus Christ, what has happened to me will turn out for my deliverance. I eagerly expect and hope that I will in no way be ashamed but will have sufficient courage so that now, as always, Christ will be exalted in my body, whether by life or by death" (Philippians 1:19).

The apostle Paul had faced death many times. He wasn't just spouting out theory; he was revealing the essence of his life.

> *For to me, to live is Christ and to die is gain. If I am to go on living in the body this will mean fruitful labor for me. Yet what shall I choose? I do not know! I am torn between the two: I desire to depart and be with Christ, which is better by far; but it is more necessary for you that I remain in the body. Convinced of this, I know that I will remain, and I will continue with all of you for your progress and joy in the faith, so that through my being with you again, your joy in Christ Jesus will overflow on account of me.*
> *– Philippians 1:21-26*

What a philosophy of life! What a profound impact that must have had on the Philippians as they read it. He was not careless or foolish. He was not stupid. Paul recognized the enormity of the things he was saying, but he was sharing out of the context of having his convictions repeatedly put to the fire. How many times had Paul been beaten, nearly drowned, starved and had his life threatened by people who could fulfill those threats? Yet he said, "For me to live is Christ and to die is gain."

Our ultimate goal is to be with Jesus forever. That is amazing! Think about it ... the God of heaven and earth, who knows all of our weaknesses, still wants to have relationship with me and you; truly His grace is overwhelming!

KNOWING I'M FORGIVEN

Do you ever feel like the enemy slimes you? I sure do. The enemy lies to us and tells us we can't come to God because we've sinned—we've been rude to a friend, cross with a child or insincere in our praise of a colleague. But even when we've committed more egregious sins, we are forgetting the most fundamental truth of our Christian lives: we are forgiven. This whole thing isn't about our sin; it's about God's righteousness.

Jesus is the basis of our salvation. If you don't understand that, the enemy will torment you your whole life. He'll get you thinking that things aren't fair or your situation isn't just. The enemy is right: it isn't just and fair for people like you and me to go to heaven forever; it's the grace and mercy of God. It's on this basis that we have fellowship and eternal life with God. If you understand that, you won't worry about the ups and downs of your life or about this or that sin. You'll just confess, live transparently, and move on.

> **This whole thing isn't about our sin; it's about God's righteousness.**

Over the years I've seen a gradual but noticeable change take place: I'm aware that I am not sinning the kind of sins that I was saved from. Are you? What I confess now is of a lesser degree, quantity, and quality of sinfulness, at least most of the time. Paradoxically, the sins I do still commit leave me more broken in the light of God's mercy and grace. Yet in the aftermath of confession and forgiveness, I stand justified nonetheless. I am one of those who are blessed, whose transgressions are forgiven, and whose sins are covered.

Blessed is the man whose sin the Lord will never count against him.

– Psalm 32:2

FREE FROM SIN

In Christ, the penalty, power, and ultimately the presence of sin has been and is being removed. There will be a time when we will be extricated from the presence of sin forever. For now we live in a diminished world, where the power of depravity still holds sway in many hearts and institutions. The good news is we no longer live connected to the penalty of this deception. I'm not a guilty man; I'm a forgiven man. My sin has been absolved.

This is not just in some distant, removed "legal" sense—I am no longer under the addictive, dominating, and dreadful power of sin. I live a victorious Christian life because even as I do things that my conscience—in its new flush of enlightenment—is speaking to me about, I immediately take those things to the Lord. "Oh God, I'm so sorry for what I just did ... for that overstatement, that ugly feeling that came toward that person." After speaking to the Father, I am free to reconcile and restore things.

> It's not that I don't sin; it's that I know what to do with sin when it raises its ugly head.

I don't live under the power of sin—I'm free from it. It's not that I don't sin; it's that I know what to do with sin when it raises its ugly head. In the midst of a continuous dialogue with the Lord, I run to Him and resolve things immediately when they spring up. In this way I live in relative freedom from sin. Get it? This is the secret to victorious living.

Sanctification is one of those religious words that we all know but probably need to spend more time pondering. I know for me that getting sanctified actually means giving up lots of comfortable little habits that God calls sin. Sometimes we go through life woefully unaware of our need for reformation and sanctification. That's often when the Holy Spirit delivers a more manifest expression of His presence. We become overjoyed at this refreshing experience with God.

Sanctified means "consecrated or set apart for the use of God." The church is the people of all time that have been set apart, separated, made holy, and justified in Christ Jesus. What an edifice God is building to His own glory as He adds to it daily through this astonishing process—calling sinners to be saints!

If you don't understand the goal of sanctification, you'll go through undue gyrations of fear and pain when harsh realities emerge in your life. The aim of sanctification is to be made more and more into the likeness of Christ in order that we may fulfill God's unique purposes for us on earth.

When we embrace all circumstances that come our way we are yielding to the process of sanctification. Banking on this reality has helped me to be unshakable. I've faced a few things in life; I'll bet you have, too. What is holiness then and how is it related to sanctification? We've been called by Christ and justified by Him. As we learn to live out of our true identities, the Holy Spirit sanctifies us. It is the Spirit's primary job to teach me how to straighten up. The result of sanctification is holiness.

In 1 Peter 1:16 Peter recounts God saying, "Be holy for I am holy." This is repeated 41 times in the Bible. It's not only an invitation; it's an empowering pronouncement. You are holy because God is holy. Walk in holiness because that's the way Jesus walks. We are meant to walk in righteousness and purity because our sins have been absolved. Jesus died for the church in order to make her holy (1 Corinthians 1:1-2) and sanctified in Him (1 Corinthians 6:11).

Two things generally happen when we have encounters with God. Most of us develop a growing hunger for the Lord as a direct consequence of His visiting, stirring, blessing, and ministering to us. Along with that, however, comes a growing awareness of our sins. To encounter God's purity is to become aware of our impurity.

How then does God go about sanctifying us? He uses the events and experiences of our ordinary lives to mold us into the image of Christ. Yet clearly for some Christians, avoidance of pain

is the highest goal in life. Tests, trials, and sufferings are seen as
aberrations from the Christian life.

However, 84 times in the New Testament Jesus said, "Follow
Me." Did He go through suffering? Did He experience pain?
Absolutely. Jesus will lead us into both pleasure and pain as we
follow Him. One way of looking at sanctification is the process of
responding to life's heartbreaks with the same grace we accord
life's pleasures and opportunities.

A LIFE OF RIGHTEOUSNESS

I am convinced that the most common reason for falling into
sin is that people do not understand their true identity and purpose as Christians. As children of God we can and should expect
the Holy Spirit to make changes in us to such an extent that our
struggle is lessened. A transformation occurs in what we desire—
righteousness—and in what we do—obeying God. It is not that
the Christian life becomes easy, but we learn to live from our center—the Holy Spirit's life in us manifests a life of righteousness.

If the old self is dead, how does sin still live in our bodies? Our
flesh still awaits redemption. Our problem is that our new nature
is tied to a body of flesh. The *flesh* (in Greek, *sarx*) is the "sin principle" at work in our lives. It is no longer our real identity as
redeemed men and women; however, this "sin principle" tries to
affect our whole being and needs to be progressively overcome.
There is a struggle to integrate our bodies with the reality of our
new nature.

When sin has affected your life, you have ample provision
through the finished work of the cross. Actions may be taken in
which sickness of spirit will be healed.

The following is a simple act of faith:

Confronting sin. Most of us are aware of our sins. When we
agree that God is right and we are wrong, we allow God's heal-

ing to access our spirits, minds, and bodies.

Confessing sin. Confession goes a step beyond acknowledging we have sinned; it is the willingness, through prayer, to admit our sins to God and receive His forgiveness.

Performing appropriate actions of repentance. Many sins require repentance to others whom we have wronged (for example, family or church members), restitution (as when we have stolen something), or a change in lifestyle (for example, in repentance from an immoral relationship).

Receiving God's forgiveness. There are many people who agree with God about their sin, confess it, and even do acts of appropriate repentance. Yet they never fully receive healing because they do not believe God has forgiven them. Receiving forgiveness requires humility, acknowledging there is nothing we can do to earn God's grace. All we can do is trust, and to do this we must acknowledge our complete dependence on God.

Forgiving others as God forgives. Jesus said, "For if you forgive men when they sin against you, your heavenly Father will also forgive your sins (Matthew 6:14-15)." God's grace has the marvelous characteristic of being inexhaustible; in fact, the more we give it away, the more it is multiplied in us. When we refuse to give away what God has so freely given us by holding people's sins against them, God's grace dries up and we develop a sickness of the spirit. Because we are all interrelated, our failure to forgive has consequences for us as well as others.

Five

The Importance of Knowing God's Word

"IT'S NOT ENOUGH TO BE BIBLICALLY LITERATE; WE MUST ALSO BE BIBLICALLY OBEDIENT."

I can imagine, as John's faith was coming alive, friends in the music business asking each other, "What is up with John?" Or even teasing John to his face: "What has gotten in to you?" What got into John was the story of Scripture culminating in Jesus. The Scripture explains captivated John's massive creative genius. John was an artist who also possessed an extraordinarily sharp, but not formally trained, theological mind. He could feel the rhythms, movements and deep human-divine drama of the New Testament stories. He was especially fond of and shaped by the Jesus he discovered in the Gospels.

It is one thing to have an orthodox theory of the inspiration of scripture, it is quite another for scripture to inspire one's life and to shape one's imagination for what it means to be a Christian and what it means to be the church. John is an example of the latter. I'm sure if pressed he could have muddled through a decent definition of the authority of Scripture, but by his life he demonstrated a love and respect of Scripture that goes way past mere Bible dictionary definition.

No one actually lives by theories or abstract moralisms; humans live by a sense of story that shapes our imaginations. One of my favorite passages in Eugene Peterson's The Message illustrates this reality. It comes from his introduction to Matthew's Gospel:

Every day we wake up in the middle of something that is already going on, that has been going on for a long time: genealogy and geology, history and culture, the cosmos—God. We are neither accidental nor incidental to the story...[From it] we get orientation, briefing, background and reassurance... [By it] we see all God's creation and salvation completed in Jesus, and all the parts of our lives—work, family, memories and dreams—are also completed in Jesus.

That completion and context—The Big Picture Story—is the dynamic that gripped and thrilled John with its vibrancy. His constant thought—shaped by the text he experienced as sacred but alive—was how he and the people he led could embody, announce and demonstrate the Gospel of the Kingdom as the Spirit-empowered, cooperative friends of Jesus on the earth today.

Todd Hunter is the former National Director of the Vineyard Churches USA and currently the director of Alpha Ministries USA.

———◆———

This is what I would refer to as the 3 M's—the Message, the Model and the Milieu. As we lead various groups and minister to different generations, there are times when the Model has to change in response to a changing landscape or Milieu, and that's fine. In fact, I think change is healthy if you are truly incarnating Jesus in your place in time.

The Message, however, remains fresh in all contexts (if it's really the Message). It is important that we understand that the Bible is the menu, not the meal. We don't worship the Scriptures, and they aren't to take the place of our worship of the Father, Son and Holy Spirit. Stick to the main and the plain themes of Scripture. We are instructed over and over again to stay with the Apostles' teaching and we have to be careful not to deviate from the Scriptures to whatever the hot new Christian fad may be at the time.

If you study church history you will see that there are no new truths, just old error. If you study church history and get that inside of you it will save you a lot of grief.

I have a prayer, and a vision: The Vineyard—and the Church at large, whatever Christian stream, tribe or family you happen to belong to— breaking through the walls of the church out into the streets and the marketplace, preaching Jesus and His Good News, accompanied by the Holy Spirit. I see the Father reaching out His hand to heal and perform miracles, and our message not ever changing from the Good News to the signs. I will die happy if that happens. The signs show He is here. The message is Jesus Christ in all His fullness—not the signs!

A few years back, I read in the newspaper about an American soldier who became separated from a daughter he fathered in the Vietnam War. The mother, a Vietnam woman, had died, and the father fled the country as the Viet Cong overtook Saigon.

He had lost all hope of ever seeing his daughter again when much to his surprise he saw her in a photograph, along with other Vietnamese Eurasian children, in a national magazine. The girl, now a teenager, looked just like him. So he wrote to her and after two years of diplomatic negotiating, they were reunited.

When I first heard this story I thought about what it must have been like the first time the girl received a letter from her father. Imagine the love, affection, and reassurance he must have poured into it and the many letters that followed. And think of what went through her mind. She had known about his existence for years, but now she began learning about the kind of person he was.

With each new letter from the United States she learned more about her father. I'm sure he also included photographs. I doubt she codified every letter, memorizing facts about her father ("he's six feet tall, blue eyes, an engineer…"). Loving relationships don't work like legal contracts. I imagine she experienced his love and concern for her through his words, and in doing so, in a small way she came to know him. She also learned about her father's purpose for her—to bring her to America so they could be together.

The Bible is analogous to that father's letters. It isn't merely a collection of "facts" about God, a celestial computer manual. It is the words of a loving Father, telling us about our relationship with Him and our divine birthright. Of course, for the girl to experience her father's love personally she had to actually meet him. The letters sustained her until she came to America, but what she got from the letters could never be compared to her later personal acquaintance with her father.

Scripture functions in a similar manner to the father's letters. The Bible is a series of letters from our heavenly Father to his children, telling us how much He loves us and how He intends to woo us through His Son, Jesus Christ.

Think of our situation this way: we're like orphans living in a far-off land, rejected by all and without hope, except for the slim possibility of being contacted by our father and rescued from captivity. But there is nothing we can do to contact him; he must find us, communicate with us, and save us. We are totally dependent on him.

Now do you understand why Christianity is called a revealed religion? The term "revelation" refers to God's self-disclosure to men and women. It is translated from a Greek noun that means "the drawing back of a veil to reveal hidden things." That's what the God of the Bible does: He reveals himself to us so that we may know Him and be redeemed by Him, and so that we may love and serve Him.

How can finite minds penetrate the maturity of an infinite God? How can the pot of clay understand the mind of the Potter? Clearly the only way we know anything about God is because He first graciously chooses to reveal Himself to us.

The Bible says that all men and women receive "general" revelation, and it is sufficient to make us aware that there is a God (see Psalms 19:1-2 and Romans 1:18-20). Nature itself and something in every human being resonates with the reality of the Divine.

But this general revelation can only go so far. While it is a powerful witness of God's presence, it fails to reveal enough of God for us to know Him intimately and by name. In other words, it is a limited self-disclosure of God, a sort of divine carrot that draws us along a path toward Jesus Christ. General revelation affords us just enough spiritual awareness to assure us that there is a God, but it cannot begin to disclose the full character and personality of this One.

General revelation prepares us for a fuller revelation, one that is rooted in the Bible and communicated through the Holy Spirit in which God reveals who He is and how we may have communion with Him. Theologians call this latter type of revelation "special revelation." It's humbling for me to realize that I can know God only if He chooses to make himself known to me! The fact that He chooses me, reveals Himself, and initiates relationship continues to astound me.

The person of Jesus Christ is the heart and apex of God's revelation (see John 1:11, 14, 18). He is the *Word* who has come in the flesh, and only those who acknowledge him as such can be saved (see 1 John 4:2).

Jesus was a real, historic figure who performed many signs and wonders that authenticated his claims, among them that he came from the Father, which was an implicit claim to deity (see John 20:30-31; Matthew 11:2-6). Do you want to know the heavenly Father? Then look at His Son, Jesus Christ, because He came to reveal His Father's nature to us (see John 14:9).

THE WRITTEN RECORD

Most Christians automatically associate the Word of God with the Bible, the Old and New Testaments. The truth is that they should, for the written record reveals the incarnate Word of God, Jesus Christ. To reach all men and women, God provided a written record of His Son.

How else could succeeding generations know about Jesus? God wanted to ensure an accurate account and authentic interpretation of His acts, so there could be no misunderstanding about His nature and how to know Him.

God crafted this in the Bible, and through this testimony all men and women may learn about and benefit from everything from God's dealings with Israel to the life of Christ. If you want to know the heavenly Father, you have to know His Son. And, if you want to know the Son and His will, you must encounter what the Bible says.

I'm making a high claim for the authority of Scripture, so it's worth asking what makes this book so special? At the same time, this raises the question of how we got the Bible.

INSPIRATION OF SCRIPTURE

Theologians say the Bible was given by inspiration, which means it is "God-breathed." But the biblical doctrine of inspiration should not be confused with the writer's inspiration. The Bible is not merely inspiring, like the writings of Dante or Shakespeare. It *is* inspired. The very words of the Old and New Testaments are the product of divine activity. The writings of the Bible are of divine origin because the authors were inspired by God; God worked through people who cooperated with Him.

Peter said:

> *Above all, you must understand that no prophecy of Scripture came about by the prophet's own interpretation. For prophecy never had its origin in the will of man, but men spoke from God as they were carried along by the Holy Spirit.*
>
> *– 2 Peter 1:20-21*

Paul wrote:

> *This is what we speak, not in words taught to us by human wisdom but in words taught by the Spirit, expressing spiritual truths in spiritual words.*
>
> *– 1 Corinthians 2:13*

Both of these passages refer to the prophets and apostles speaking by inspiration, but this also includes the message that they wrote.

Paul related truth to questions and problems which are just as pertinent in today's world. He addressed divisiveness, immaturity, instability, divisions, jealousy, envy, lawsuits, questionable ethics, marital difficulties, sexual immorality, church problems, misuse of spiritual gifts, and concern for the future. Over 16 times Paul used the formula "know ____" and then pointed them to the truths that would help them with their questions and problems.

A common analogy for how inspiration works is a sailboat and the wind. The Holy Spirit, like the wind, filled the sails of the writers. Without the wind, the boat could go nowhere. However, like all analogies, this one breaks down when pushed too far. For example, a sailboat is an impersonal, inanimate object; human beings are intensely personal, flesh and blood agents of revelation.

God didn't merely dictate the Bible to writer-secretaries, as though human authors had no more a part in producing Scripture than the computer on which I write this article. No, the Bible is the Word of God spoken through human writers, and as such it bears the marks of humanity: God's truth communicated in the authors' unique language and culture. This dynamic is captured in 2 Samuel 23:2: "The Spirit of the Lord spoke through me; his word was on my tongue."

Both the Holy Spirit and human beings are involved with writing Scripture. Nevertheless, the critical element was the Holy

Spirit; His presence ensured that what was written was wholly true—true in the ways of God's choosing and not in the ways always acceptable to modern men and women.

Many people find it difficult to accept the whole Bible as the Word of God. Some believe parts of the Bible are in error; they retain the right to pick and choose only those passages they agree with. Thomas Jefferson removed every verse from his Bible that referred to the supernatural! Others believe the Bible "contains" the Word of God and that it is the Word of God only to the extent that we experience God in reading it. Let's examine these approaches.

INTERPRETING SCRIPTURE

As the church we all have the privilege and responsibility to interpret Scripture, to hear its message of God to us. In this process, however, I believe that there are some important things that are often overlooked.

The most important facet to keep in mind, I think, is the fact that Scripture originally came to a people in a unique time period, mindset, and culture. The backdrop through which God has spoken in recorded Scripture is different—sometimes strikingly so—from our own. It behooves the reader, then, to be ever mindful that Scripture was written to a people who understood it. What they understood is of primary value for us. To grasp what the original recipients received is one of the highest goals in the interpretation of Scripture.

By contrast, one of the most distressing things in many contemporary church circles is the purely subjective way Scripture is often handled. We hear statements such as, "In our study we are going to put the Word of God first. We are not dealing with what we think it says, but with what it actually says." The implication of this statement is that any different interpretation is based on "what people think," while the one being taught is the "plain meaning"!

While the plain meaning of the text is the goal of interpretation, often what is arrived at is not the plain meaning. Dr. Gordon Fee, a noted New Testament scholar, has stated that the phrase "plain meaning" should be understood as having to do with the author's original intent, which would have been plain to those whom the message had originally been given. Plain meaning does not directly relate with how someone from this culture in the late twentieth century reads his own cultural values into the text through the distorted prism of seventeenth century language.

This obvious distortion is rooted in a collective worldview. There are those who contend that Scripture is to be received and interpreted in a purely subjective way, thinking this is somehow "more spiritual" than social and cultural exegesis. I think the problem with this is readily apparent; the Word of God stands as an objective body of truth, regardless of how I may assign it a "plain meaning" through my subjective responses.

Let me illustrate this phenomenon with an example many can relate with. One of the most emphasized teachings in the church today is the teaching on faith. It is an often-taught subject because of its relevance to living a Christian life. Our truest desire is to please God, and Scripture informs us that it is impossible to please God without faith. There is a much-popularized teaching about the subject within the church. It is unfortunate that when we popularize a subject, we often lose sight of its historical meaning in Scripture. I have no problem with some of this popularized teaching on faith. On the other hand, I often

> **Our truest desire is to please God, and Scripture informs us that it is impossible to please God without faith.**

question the hermeneutical procedures and some of the conclusions drawn as a result. Let me suggest how I understand some of the passages of Scripture which are used in relationship to the prayer of faith.

Mark 11:20-24 is used to support the idea of what is commonly called positive confession:

> *In the morning, as they went along, they saw the fig tree withered from the roots. Peter remembered and said to Jesus, "Rabbi, look! The fig tree you cursed has withered!"*
>
> *"Have faith in God," Jesus answered. "I tell you the truth, if anyone says to this mountain, 'Go, throw yourself into the sea,' and does not doubt in his heart but believes that what he says will happen, it will be done for him. Therefore I tell you, whatever you ask for in prayer, believe that you have received it, and it will be yours."*

If you will claim what you have asked God for, the popular teaching goes, God will surely give it to you. The assumption is that faith is supported and illustrated by the activity of claiming in the now what has not yet been fulfilled in the same dimension of time. This often puts us in a position of appearing foolish, in that we are stating in the present tense language something that is not yet fulfilled.

I understand this passage differently, however. I think verse 22 should be translated as follows: "You have the faithfulness of God." You will notice that I have translated the passage with the words of God, as compared to in God. God's faithfulness guides us to God's ends, in God's timing ... not ours.

THE CHARACTERISTICS OF SCRIPTURE

So what are the characteristics of the Bible that set it apart from all other books?

For centuries Christian theologians have used several terms to summarize a high view of biblical inspiration. Some of these terms were used to combat false teachers who were undermining the authority of the Bible. Others were drawn directly from Scripture itself. Let's take a closer look at them.

Infallible. This means Scripture will never deceive us; it will never lead us astray. It is wholly trustworthy and wholly reliable. It contains no mistakes and is incapable of error. Psalm 19:7 say, "The law of the Lord is perfect, reviving the soul. The statutes of the Lord are trustworthy, making wise the simple." God cannot lie (Titus 1:2), so His Word will not mislead us. Think of it this way: If God cannot lie, then how could He lie in His Word?

Inerrant. The Bible is also wholly true. What the Bible says, God says. God speaks through the human writers yet it is without error. In 1776 John Wesley wrote, "If there be any mistakes in the Bible, there may well be a thousand. If there be one falsehood in that Book, it did not come from the God of truth."

The idea of inerrancy comes from the attitude that Christ had toward Scripture, which was one of total trust, and it comes from Scripture itself: "I, the Lord, speak the truth; I declare what is right" (Isaiah 45:19; Proverbs 30:5-6). This isn't to say that an error in Scripture would destroy belief in Christ's deity, the resurrection, or any other cardinal truth of Christianity. However, it would undermine our confidence that the Bible is wholly true, a trustworthy authority and guide in all matters of faith and practice. I am first to admit that many Christians more mature than I do not believe in an inerrant Bible. Further, inerrancy is not the basis for church membership or fellowship. But nonetheless, I have found biblical inerrancy as I have outlined it here to be essential to living a consistent Christian life; it removes all doubt surrounding the reliability and authority of the Bible in all matters of faith and practice.

Plenary. Plenary inspiration means the Bible is full, complete, un-qualified. As Paul explains in Romans 15:4, "Everything that was written in the past was written to teach us, so that through endurance and encouragement of the Scriptures we might have hope." This means all of Scripture is inspired.

Verbal. Inspiration extends to the words of Scripture themselves and not only to the ideas. Because inspiration is verbal, we know objectively who God is.

Clarity. The Bible is clear enough for us to read and understand it. Psalm 119:105 says, "Your Word is a lamp unto my feet and a light unto my path." This doesn't mean every passage in the Bible is easy to understand, but there is enough clarity to live by. Augustine, a fourth-century bishop and probably the greatest theologian in church history, said, "In the clear passages of Scripture, everything is found that pertains to faith and life."

Sufficient. Clark Pinnock says, "To confess sufficiency and clarity is just to affirm that Scripture contains enough light to save sinners and direct the church." In 2 Timothy 3:15 Paul reminds Timothy that the Scriptures "are able to make you wise for salvation through faith in Christ Jesus." This is not to say that the Bible exhausts all possible or even all actual revelation (John 21:25) or that it reveals everything that can be known about God (1 Corinthians 13:12). This means that modern revelations from God are not to be placed on a level equal to Scripture in authority; they are not to be used as yardsticks for judging other revelation. In other words, any source of "revelation" that contradicts Scripture is to be rejected.

Efficacy. Finally, Scripture is effective in bringing people to a personal relationship with Christ. The Word of God generates eternal life. Peter says, "For you have been born again, not of perishable seed, but of imperishable, through the living and enduring Word of God" (1 Peter 1:23). Through the power of the Holy Spirit, it also creates saving faith. It overcomes unbelief and promotes salvation (Romans 10:17), judging and piercing our innermost being. "For the Word of God is living and active.

Sharper than any double-edged sword, it penetrates even to dividing soul and spirit, joints and marrow; it judges the thoughts and attitudes of the heart" (Hebrews 4:12). This passage highlights the dynamic Word of God, a living power that judges as an all-seeing eye, penetrating a person's most innermost being.

CONSERVATORS

Earlier in this chapter, I compared the Bible with an American GI's letters to his long-lost Vietnamese daughter. For two years she received letters while he tried to get her released from Vietnam. I imagine that she saved every letter he sent, re-reading them daily, wondering about the meaning behind some sentences. They were, without question, the most precious objects she owned. We are called to conserve the Bible in a similar way, for in so doing we guard God's truth and maintain our relationship with Him.

The great leaders of the church have always been conservators of God's Word. For example, Augustine wrote, "Do not follow my writings as Holy Scripture. When you find in Holy Scripture anything you did not believe in before, believe it without doubt; but in my writings, you should hold nothing for certain."

Luther, the great reformer, said, "We must make a great difference between God's Word and the word of man. A man's word is a little sound, that flies into the air, and soon vanishes; but the Word of God is greater than heaven and earth, yea, greater than heaven and hell, for it forms part of the power of God, and endured everlastingly."

The most significant aspect of my calling is preaching the Word of God. For, when any activity in the Christian life is separated from God's truth, it soon loses its power and leads us away from the Gospel.

Of course, the Vietnamese girl also probably told everyone she came in contact with about her father. Can't you see her reading sections from the letters to friends and strangers, showing them his picture and describing in detail what she knew about his home and occupation? Nobody could meet her without learning something about her father because the letters were lifelines to a living relationship.

Again, the analogy to the Christian and the Bible is striking, for we are called to be communicators as well as conservators of God's Word. I preach the Gospel, teach, worship, feed the poor, house the homeless, pray for the sick, prophecy, and so on, because the Bible says that's what lovers of God do!

Conservation and communication go together. To fail to combine the Word of God with the works of the Spirit is to hold something less than a high view of Scripture. Jesus said, "If anyone loves me, he will obey my teaching. My Father will love him, and we will come to him and make our home with him. He who does not love me will not obey my teaching" (John 14:23-24).

DEVOTION TO THE BOOK

Devoting ourselves to the apostles teaching—as in Acts 2:42—does not just mean reading the book. It means conforming to the book. What most people think of as "Bible teaching" isn't Bible teaching at all. It isn't how many pages you cover or how many outlines you have; it isn't even how many verses you have memorized. It is not how much you're "in the Bible;" what really counts is how much Bible is in you at the end of the day!

It is not how much you're "in the Bible;" what really counts is how much Bible is in you at the end of the day!

Do you think like the Bible? Do you write checks like the Bible? Do you spend your hours like the Bible? Is your life centered in the God of this book? Are you letting "the word of Christ dwell in you richly as you teach and admonish one another with all wisdom" (Colossians 3:16a)?

Keep your focus on walking like Jesus, inculcating the life of Christ in your life, deepening your prayer life and fellowship, strengthening your commitment and interdependence on one another. If revival doesn't result in these behaviors—giving to the poor and sharing our faith—is it truly revival? Let's become like the saints in the wake of Pentecost, a people devoted. They were as devoted to being a community as they were to their own personal growth.

The Bible is unlike any other book. It is a collection of incredible love letters from God, telling us about our relationship with him. Small wonder that we are called to be men and women of The Book, meditating on God's Word and allowing it to transform our minds, hearts, souls, and actions.

Why Worship

"IF YOU WANT TO KNOW WHAT YOU WORSHIP, ASK
YOURSELF, 'WHERE DO I SPEND MY TIME? MY MONEY? MY
ENERGY?' THAT WILL TELL YOU WHAT YOU WORSHIP."

One of the biggest things that stands out in my mind about John Wimber's heart for worship is the way he jealously guarded God's glory. Coming from the music industry, John had been around all sorts of self-promoting musicians. He was very sensitive to the issue of showmanship versus worship. Worship music was to be Christ-centered, not man-centered.

Whenever the focus became the music rather than the Lord, it made John uncomfortable. He strongly valued the activity of the Holy Spirit in the midst of worship, and the importance of being sensitive to God. John always led us to come to worship with an expectation to meet with God rather than putting on a show.

Andy Park is a former worship leader and pastor at Vineyard Anaheim, in California. Andy and his wife, Linda, lead a Vineyard church in Surrey, B.C. Canada.

———◆———

I was seven years old when I first came across the Vineyard values in worship. John Wimber and a big team showed up in Chorleywood, England, where I lived, and my Mum took me along to a couple of the meetings. More than anything I was struck by how "real" it all seemed. There was a strong sense of "encounter" – the people of God, in the presence of God, pouring out the praises of God. They sang with faith, knowing that their songs could reach the heart of Almighty God. They sang with expectation that they might even draw near to their heavenly Father through these simple choruses they uttered. I'm not sure I could have explained it like this at the time, but looking back those couple of meetings had a profound effect on how me – and still now affect how I worship Jesus.

Matt Redman is a worship leader and songwriter, serving with Soul Survivor in the United Kingdom.

———◆———

THE FLAME OF GOD'S PRESENCE

by Carol Wimber

I was raised Roman Catholic. As Catholics, we knew that one way we could always tell the "True Church" from the "non-Catholic" churches (the only two denominations in our minds), was the small red flame in the oil lamp up near the altar. This was in every Catholic church in the world. That flame signified that the manifest Presence of God was there in the Consecrated Host, kept behind the doors and veils of the small "Tabernacle" on the altar. It was reassuring to us Catholic children when we would go into an unfamiliar church and see the flame burning. We knew we were safe. ... We hadn't somehow stumbled into a non-Catholic, heathen, perhaps even Protestant building. The flame was right up there, plain as day for us to see. It was a sign to us.

The flame burned night and day, every day. If the flame ever had gone out, we as young children expected that we would all drop dead, right there on the spot! The beautiful stained glass windows wouldn't have meant anything. It wouldn't have mattered if it was the cathedral where the Archbishop was. The beautifully sculptured crucifix and the statues of the saints and martyrs would have offered no comfort.

To us, the extinguishing of the flame would have meant that the Presence of God in Jesus was no longer with us. Down the road several years, we brought the first ministry team of teenagers to St. Michael's Le'Belfrey in York, England. It was 1981. John and I had been praying together for the meeting that evening when the Lord gave me a word from 2 Chronicles 29:27-28:

Hezekiah gave the order to sacrifice the burnt offering on the altar. As the offering began, singing to the Lord began also, accompanied by trumpets and the instruments of David king of Israel. The whole assembly bowed in worship, while the singers sang and the trumpeters played. All this continued until the sacrifice of the burnt offering was completed.

John would always refer to this word as "the time in York when God gave him that word." However it happened, that evening the Holy Spirit began to move in a tremendously powerful way. Blind eyes saw, the deaf ears heard, and the lame walked. The whole while a young boy sang in the influence of the Spirit. A boy around 13 or 14 years old was just standing there when the Holy Spirit fell. The Spirit fell on him and he raised up his head and began to sing in the Spirit. He continued singing without a pause for the entire hour or so that the Lord was manifesting His presence with signs, wonders, and healings. He didn't stop singing until it was all done.

John and I understood that night, that for us, the Vineyard, that song and singing would always be attached to the presence and manifestation of the Holy Spirit. So when I think and pray about the state of the Vineyard, I listen to the songs that come forth from the churches and I weigh our condition by them. Is Jesus still giving us His song? I take comfort in this.

If the songs ever dry up, I'll be distressed as if I were a child again in my Catholic church if the flame had gone out on the altar. That will be the sign to me that we have lost our way. I hope that those of us who pray will not wait until some obvious disaster takes place, or some quiet deadly paralysis that accompanies the end of movements that were started by fire from Heaven.

Men cry out under a load of oppression; they plead for relief from the arm of the powerful. But no one says, "Where is God my Maker, who gives songs in the night?" (Job 35:9-10).

Many of you are too young to remember how beautiful the

Catholic Charismatic movement was, and the sweet, simple, God-hungry songs that came from that outpouring. But I remember. A few of you remember and maybe were a part of the Jesus Movement and the wonderful songs that came through them; we still sing them today. But I don't ever want to go into the monument stage—I want to rend the heavens! You see, for me, songs that Jesus gives you for His church is that flame next to the altar that assures me that Jesus' manifest presence is still here with us.

(Adapted from the Vineyard Music Songwriters Gathering, February 1998.)

THE VINEYARD AND WORSHIP

Worship was perhaps the first thing God told us to do and then He had to teach us how. It's not new anymore and that's good, but it sure was new to us all those years ago when we first started meeting in a house after evening church. God took us by the hands and taught us to walk (see Hosea 11:3), giving us the simple instruction to sing to Him and not just about Him. This was revolutionary to us: singing songs straight to Jesus. We sang love songs to Jesus, and it was this intimacy that broke us down.

You can still keep a certain reserve intact singing theological songs about the faith. These songs are wonderful and I'm thankful for every one of them. But when you sing, "You Bless Me Lord Forever" or "Whom Have I But You?", it breaks through to your inner being and expresses what your spirit needs to say.

It wasn't everyone's cup of tea, of course. Much of the church was not comfortable with such deep intimacy, but we were instructed by the Lord to worship Him this way: "Sing to Him, sing praise to Him" (1 Chronicles 16:9).

We would worship God for a long time, as long as we wanted, wherever we wanted; we would worship first and we would worship at the end. A meeting of two or three was reason to worship, and we worshiped in the airport on our way to bring a worship team to another country; and many times we got in trouble because we were late for meetings due to the team worshiping.

We worshiped God because He is worthy. To worship is the only adequate response to who Jesus is and what He has done for us. Whenever we worship Jesus we are not alone even if we are alone. Let me explain.

There is a party going on all the time around Jesus:

> *But you have come to Mount Zion, to the heavenly Jerusalem, the city of the living God. You have come to thousands upon thousands of angels in joyful assembly, to the Church of the Firstborn, whose names are written in heaven. You have come to God, the judge of all men, to the spirits of righteous men made perfect, to Jesus the mediator of a new covenant.*
>
> *– Hebrews 12:22-24*

Now this shouldn't be taken lightly. We are invited to the only real party. When we worship, we are there! Think about it: Angels, elders, living creatures, cloud of witnesses, spirits of righteous people made perfect and Jesus Himself!

You want to go to that party? "Then let us be thankful, and so worship God acceptably with reverence and awe, for 'our God is a consuming fire'" (Hebrews 12:28-29).

WORSHIP IS OUR ADMISSION TICKET

We must worship because we are body and spirit. Just as we need to nurture our body by giving it food and drink, worship feeds and refreshes our spirit. Vineyard Worship is all over the world now and it changed the face of the church. People used to be called "song leaders," but now they're called "worship leaders."

Many years ago when we were baby Christians and John was out of work, Christmas was approaching and we were out of money. The Lord told John to quit his job, so he quit. Soon after he quit, he was offered a good paying position at Disney, placing their different bands and groups—something John would have been good at. But Sheldon, our pastor, didn't think this was a good plan (being part of the entertainment industry again), so John declined the offer.

Months had gone by and we had nothing until one evening, Bill Medley called from the U.K. where their band, the Righteous Brothers, had gone with the Beatles as a warm up group, and Bill wanted John to produce a Christmas album. John would have loved to do that, and not only that, but he could have total freedom to do it any way he wanted. It seemed perfect, and an answer to our prayers: they would send us a $5,000 deposit right away! John said he would call him back.

He told me what was going on and asked me what I thought, and I wanted him to take it just because we needed the money. In my heart, though, I also thought it could be a trap. John thought so too, like the devil was trying to buy him back. We prayed, and John called back Bill's wife because he didn't have the strength to talk to Bill himself. And John told her to thank Bill for the offer, but he wasn't able to do it.

It was then that he went out and got a job at a machine shop. I don't know what they manufactured, but I do know that two men got their hands crushed in the machines on the job. And here was John, a musician. He was cleaning the oil drums when an old friend came by and asked where his office was. John had to admit that the oil drum was his office and the guy just looked at John in horror and disgust. "What are you doing here man? Have you lost your mind?" John said, "Yes, I have lost my mind and don't ever plan on getting it back."

He sold all his horns, except one, which he saved to trade for a painting he knew I wanted. That Saturday, he went through every closet, every cupboard, and every shelf where he kept his lifetime of work. He then cleared off the piano and cleaned out the piano bench. All of his award winning arrangements, jazz records, and reference records. He took his wonderful music—years of work— and he placed it all in cardboard boxes and loaded them into our station wagon and drove up to the garbage dump on the mountain. He opened the back of the wagon and started pushing those boxes out the rear of the car ... shoving them out with his foot.

A lifetime of work, sinking down into the mud and garbage. He didn't talk at all. He didn't say anything. My heart ached for him, but I've never been more proud to be his wife than I was right then. I prayed silently that God would do something beautiful someday through John and music that would be pleasing to God. And I recalled this verse:

> *I tell you the truth unless a kernel of wheat falls to the ground and dies, it remains only a single seed. But if it dies, it produces many seeds.*
>
> *– John 12:24*

That is what I believed has happened. I believe the seeds of worship were planted in the Vineyard when John's music sunk in the mud of the garbage dump. It was total and complete abandonment to the will of God!

———◆———

A LIFESTYLE OF WORSHIP

I took my seat on the couch a few minutes late. When I looked around the softly lit room, no one looked back. Eyes were closed, postures relaxed, a few were seated, some knelt and two women stood with their hands turned upward. The guitar strummed softly and played the same three chords over and over again as each member of this little gathering in Yorba Linda, California, sang to the Lord.

They seemed to sing forever. *What was the point?* I thought. *Weren't we there to study the Bible?*

I felt the heat rise in my cheeks; my palms became sweaty; and I was embarrassed by the intimate language of the songs being played. *Lord, am I supposed to sing to you like that too?* I certainly hoped not!

Yet within a few weeks, I felt my heart soften. I was caught off-guard by the power of the lyrics in those songs. Tears rolled down my cheeks as the music played. My mind couldn't comprehend what my heart was experiencing. Singing those sweet simple love songs to the Lord led me into personal revival.

Intimate worship transformed my life as a Christian. In fact, what I experienced in this small group became the foundation for the Vineyard movement. The Lord's reviving presence in us spilled over into the lives of tens of thousands of people over the next 25 years, and it continues to this day.

God has been stirring the church in an unprecedented manner. The past century has been characterized by renewal. As with any flood; however, there is danger of being overwhelmed by the strength of the current. The flow needs to be channeled in order to be effective.

In living a Christ-centered life, I see four banks providing the necessary boundaries for the greatest benefit to come from this flood we call renewal: Worship, Word, Walk, and Works. These banks not only direct the flow of renewal, but they also intensify its force.

One of the rich gifts that the Holy Spirit imparted to the church in the past century is a love for worship. Because of the Bible's availability, laymen for the first time were able to transform the Scriptures into lyrical adoration and musical expressions of worship. This has resulted in a grassroots proliferation of simple, heartfelt worship music like never before.

Remembering my first visit to that little gathering in Yorba Linda, California that eventually became the foundation for the Vineyard movement, there were many things that made me a bit uncomfortable.

I have this theory: That every little act done because I love Jesus counts. It counts as worship. To use the illustration of marriage, as Paul's letter Ephesians talks about, I believe that making love is the culmination of the love relationship that has been going on all day, every day. All the many different expressions of life that have preceded the actual act give it meaning and worth.

In the same way, I believe that when we gather and express our worship, it is all the expressions of love and devotion that have gone on before that make worship meaningful. Otherwise our worship can be as it is described in Isaiah 29:13:

> *The Lord says: "These people come near to me with their mouth and honor me with their lips, but their hearts are far from me. Their worship of me is made up only of rules taught by men."*

Let me explain this further, by giving you a few other illustrations such as hair, perfume, and pierced ears. We have two choices: either we can worship our way, in the flesh, or Jesus' way, in the Spirit. John 12:3 recounts:

> *Then Mary took about a pint of pure nard, and expensive perfume; she poured it on Jesus' feet and wiped His feet with her hair. And the house was filled with the fragrance of the perfume.*

Every time I choose to do things God's way and resist my way, I think my spirit is kneeling in front of Jesus and I am pouring sweet perfume on His feet and wiping them with my hair.

Is this kind of abandonment you experience? Or are you still wanting your rights, your needs met, or to be treated fairly? I gave up my rights for His. I have no rights.

Our entire life can be worship to God. All the pain and the times of sorrow can be surrendered in an act of worship with just as much value as the spontaneous praise and gratitude that goes up when we experience the joy and blessings of life.

Every act of obedience is worship. Every time we choose another over ourselves, it is an act of worship. Every time we decide to lay our own way down in favor of Jesus' way, is an act of worship. After all that, the real question arises: Is this what God meant when He told us to worship our God with our whole mind, strength, heart and body?

> **Every step you take, every breath of every day, you are making the choice whether you realize it or not.**

The word, worship in its simplest form means "to serve," and the question I'm asking is, "Who are you going to serve?" It reminds me of Bob Dylan's song, *Ya Gotta Serve Somebody*.

As you live out your life, who are you going to serve? In the hundreds of little choices you make every day, who are you choosing to serve? Every step you take, every breath of every day, you are making the choice whether you realize it or not.

You got up this morning and started making these choices. Will I be kind to my spouse, my sister, and my neighbor and thereby give my worship to God, or will I consider myself the most important person in the exchanges and therefore worship myself?

Will I joyfully give in to inconvenience when it's required as an act of worship, or will I demand my place and worship myself?

Will I love even when the other is unlovable and let that be an act of worship? Or will I "Amen" the spirit of this world and make my life's pursuit reaching my full potential?

If we worship Jesus, serving Him, then our every act and thought has meaning. Acts of kindness are not just little niceties; they become acts of worship. Bagging food for the poor because "I was hungry and you gave me food" is worship.

Every time you make the decision to walk in truth and humility, every time you put someone else ahead of you, every time you decide to pray for someone who has hurt or offended you instead of hating them, it is an act of worship. It's all worship! Whatever I do for "the least of these, my brethren," I am doing for Jesus.

So, if my marriage is difficult, or my boss is impossible, or my parents are unreasonable, that's OK, because I can still be a good husband, a good employee, or a good son if I am actually living out my life before God and for His approval and pleasure, rather than looking for satisfaction in the here and now.

The perfume Mary poured out was equivalent to a years' salary. Think about this for a moment: She showed such a lavish display of worship. Was it merely an emotional catharsis that would be gone when her emotions led her in a different way?

"Therefore, when Christ came into the world, he said: 'Sacrifice and offering you did not desire, but a body you prepared for me; with burnt offering and sin offerings you were not pleased. Then I said, 'Here I am – it is written about me in the scroll – I have come to do your will, O God" (Hebrews 10:5-7). This echoes an earlier Psalm:

> *Sacrifice and offering you did not desire, but my ears you have pierced, burnt offerings and sin offerings you did not require. Then I said, 'Here I am, I have come. It is written about me in the scroll. I desire to do your will, O My God, your law is within my heart.*
>
> *– Psalm 40:6-7*

Here David prophesies about Jesus, and the author of Hebrews takes this up, talking about Jesus and His attitude of worship towards His Father: "I have come to do your will, not my will but yours be done."

What does the reference mean, piercing the ear? It was a sign that you belonged to another, and your life was no longer your own. It meant that you have a master you love and you chose to live with him instead of going out on your own.

Look at Exodus 21:5-6:

> *But if the servant declares, "I love my master and my wife and children and do not want to go free," then his master must take him before the judges. He shall take him to the door or the doorpost and pierce his ear with an awl. Then he will be his servant for life.*

It's servanthood and it's a lifestyle of choosing to worship. You live your life out before God in every area, responding to His direction. Worship—besides being the instinctual response to our Savior—is also the main means of grace wherewith Christ feeds our spirit. We open our spirit to the Spirit all day, every day, as the Lord pours His life into us. God's life is the only life.

Are you hungry? Are you thirsty? Are you empty and lonely? Worship God, and allow Him to fill you up over and over again.

Have you ever thought that maybe it didn't matter that much how you live? Perhaps you could sin around a bit and the affects would be gone and over within a few days? When you bow down to Satan by giving in to temptation, this too is worship, which is serving his purposes.

> *Therefore, I urge you, brothers, in view of God's mercy, to offer your bodies as living sacrifices, holy and pleasing to God. This is your spiritual act of worship. Do not be conformed any longer to the patterns of this world, but be transformed by the renewing of your mind.*
>
> *– Romans 12:1-2*

Worship is how you live. It's where and how you spend your time and your money. Worship manifests in obedience. As you worship in obedience, your life here has meaning and purpose. This is called a lifestyle of worship to the King!

Intimate worship has forever transformed my life as a Christian. As a result, it is an integral part of where we have been and where we are going in our local church body. Additionally, I have always made it a point in the Vineyard movement that worship must be our first priority.

Becoming true worshippers is the chief assignment God has given us in this lifetime. God is bringing the church to her knees to teach her how to express in intimate, loving, adoring language, her love for Him and her appreciation of His blessing and loving care.

In addition to what we tend to define as worship—singing and music—the Lord calls us to live a life of worship. The Word, our walk with Christ, and the works of the church as a whole are all expressions of worship. They necessarily flow out of a heart that is devoted to adoring the Lord.

Worship is not about personality, temperament, personal limitations, church background, or comfort; it's about God. We are called to worship for His benefit, not ours. Yet in God's grace we do indeed benefit greatly when we give ourselves to worshipping

God. We've been designed to worship, and it is our destiny.

In John 4:23, Jesus addresses a Samaritan woman by showing her the heart of the Father as regards to worship. He says,

> *A time is coming and has now come when the true worshippers will worship the Father in Spirit and truth; for they are the kind of worshippers the Father seeks. Our Father is and has been actively seeking worshippers since He created Adam and Eve.*

Right at the heart of this message is that God is calling a people out for Himself to worship Him. Please understand: this is not some kind of ego trip because poor old God has a bad self-image. He doesn't need to be buttered up by the loving things we say.

Quite the opposite is true. God knows that the greater good in all eternity is Himself. Learning this truth and expressing it to God causes us to draw near to Him as the source of all blessing.

As we discover and experience the majesty of God, the reality of His presence in our lives, and His availability to us in our times of need, we will be unable to keep from worshipping Him. It is a natural and forgone response.

WORSHIP UNPACKED

The most significant lesson that Carol and the early Vineyard fellowship learned was that worship is the act of freely giving love to God. Indeed, in the Psalms we read, "I love you, O Lord, my strength" (Psalm 18:1). Worship is also an expression of awe, submission, and respect toward God:

> *Come, let us sing for joy to the Lord; let us shout aloud to the Rock of our salvation. Let us come before Him with thanksgiving and extol Him with music and song.*
> *— Psalm 95:1-2*

Sing to the Lord a new song; sing to the Lord, all the earth.
Sing to the Lord, praise His name, and proclaim His salva-
tion day after day. Declare His glory among the nations, his
marvelous deeds among all peoples.

– Psalm 96:1-3

Our heart's desire should be to worship God; God has designed us all for His purpose. If we don't worship God, we will worship something or someone else. It is our instinct. We delight in our God, and when we worship Him, He delights and sings over us, and that gives us joy.

The Lord your God is in your midst, a victorious warrior.
He will exalt over you with joy, he will quiet you with his
love, he will rejoice over you with singing.

– Zephaniah 3:17 (NASB)

But how should we worship God? There are various ways described in the Old and New Testament:

Adoration – praising God for simply who He is—Lord of the universe.

Thanksgiving – giving thanks to God for what He has done, especially for His works of creation and salvation.

Confession – the acknowledgement of sin and guilt to a holy and righteous God.

As Carol would point out, worship involves not only our thought and intellect, but also our body. The Scriptures are packed with a dizzying variety of praise expressions including singing, playing instruments, dancing, kneeling, bowing down, raising our hands, and so on. These are all aspects of true worship.

When we acknowledge the greatness of God and His permeating presence in all creation, we become aware of our own limitations. The discovery drives us to worship, as it should. The late

19th-century Archbishop of Canterbury William Temple said, "To worship is to quicken the conscience by the holiness of God, to feed the mind with the truth of God, to purge the imagination by the beauty of God, to open the heart to the love of God and to devote the will to the purpose of God."

Can you see how all-encompassing worship is? It is here that God is enthroned by our praises. The enthroning process is one in which we readily admit that He is God and we are not. Our praises remind us of God's holiness, truth, and beauty. We lift up the Lord to His proper place in our lives when we devote ourselves to His leadership and love. This exercise is not merely a church ritual, but a necessary discipline and privilege. We are changed when we worship.

I used to love to sing a little chorus I learned in church years ago when I was first converted called, "Turn Your Eyes upon Jesus" penned by Helen Lemmel. Its refrain beautifully illustrates the power of worshipping the Lord and the impact it has on our lives:

Turn your eyes upon Jesus,
Look full in His wonderful face,
And the things of earth will grow strangely dim,
In the light of His glory and grace.

As we interact with God, we will find ourselves more and more satisfied in Him and less and less satisfied with the things that have attracted or enticed us in the past.

THE IMPORTANCE OF WORSHIP IN HEAVEN

This isn't even all of it! We're on our way to heaven. This life is not our final destination. We live in a cocoon; we have not yet emerged as butterflies. The real thing is going on in heavenly realms. However, God wants us to begin our eternal relationship with Him here on this earth. When we do, we bring others into relationship with Him as well. That's what this life is all about.

God is calling, wooing, and instructing His people to worship, worship, and worship! He expects us to worship at the drop of a hat. Worship with a flat tire, worship when you get bad news from the bank, worship all the time, because that's what we're made for and that's what we'll be doing from now on. This is just the rehearsal, not the play.

When Jesus taught the Lord's Prayer, He was saying in a prophetic sense to pray that the Father accomplishes on earth what He has already established in heaven.

That's what we're waiting for as Christians; we're waiting for Jesus to culminate the Kingdom; to fulfill His promises and bring heaven to earth.

One of the ways that God is preparing the church for His coming is by teaching her to worship. There is an unprecedented hunger for fresh musical expressions of love for the Lord among most Christians. Churches all over the world have reinvested value in the portion of their gatherings devoted to worship. This can be seen in the growing interest in live worship bands as well as longer worship sessions.

All these signs translate into a greater anticipation of Jesus' coming. We know the Lord now through our worship, but we long to know Him as He is, as we will when He returns for His bride.

PHASES IN THE HEART

It is helpful to understand not only why and how we are to worship God, but also what happens when we worship God.

There are five basic phases of worship, phases through which leaders attempt to find the congregation. Understanding these phases is helpful in our experience of God. Keep in mind that as we pass through these phases we are headed toward one goal: intimacy with God.

I define intimacy as belonging to or revealing one's deepest nature to another, in this case to God. This intimacy is marked by close association, presence, and contact.

The first phase is the call to worship, which is a message directed toward the people or toward God. It is an invitation to worship. This might be accomplished through a song like, *Come let Us Worship and Bow Down* or it may be jubilant such as through the song, *Don't You Know It's Time to Praise the Lord?* The underlying thought of the call to worship is "Let's do it, let's worship God now." Song selection for the call to worship is quite important, for this sets the tone for the gathering, and directs people to God.

The second phase is the engagement, which is the electrifying dynamic of connection to God and to each other. Expressions of love, adoration, praise, jubilation, intercession, petition—all of the dynamics of prayer interlocked with worship—come forth from one's heart. In the engagement phase we praise God for who He is through music as well as prayer.

The third phase is moving more into a loving and more intimate language. Being in God's presence excites our hearts and minds as we want to praise God for the deeds He has done, for how He has moved in history, for His character and attributes.

This kind of intimacy often causes us to meditate, even as we are singing about our relationship with the Lord. Not only is it helpful to understand why and how we are to worship God, it is also helpful to understand what happens when we worship God.

The fourth phase is our expression in worship. Physical and emotional expression in worship can result in dance and body movement. This is an appropriate response to God if the church is on that crest. It is most inappropriate if it is whipped up or if the focal point is on the dance rather than on the true jubilation in the Lord. We have expressed what is in our hearts and in our bodies, and now it is time to wait for God to respond. Stop talking and wait for Him to speak, to move. The almighty God visits His people! When we cultivate stillness as a part of our worship time together, we are enriched by the deep communion that can take place.

The church must be quickened to the fact that the God of the universe will visit us if we but worship Him in Spirit and Truth. Much of the time when Christians come together they don't expect God to do much, but God is like an anxious bridegroom outside the bride's door. And we, as the bride, frequently forget what we gather for because we are scattered in our thoughts or preoccupied with concerns.

We should expect the Spirit of God to work among us. He moves in different ways—sometimes for salvation, sometimes for deliverance, sometimes for sanctification or healing, and sometimes just to dwell with us in fellowship. The Spirit of God is most willing and desires to visit us.

God also visits through prophetic gifts. Oftentimes the most prophetic people are too timid to speak up. The Spirit of God visits us through Spirit-inspired Scripture containing a prophetic meaning for that moment. We need to learn to wait on the Lord and let Him speak in our midst.

The fifth phase of worship is giving of substance. The church knows so little about giving, yet the Bible exhorts us to give to God. It is pathetic to see people preparing for ministry who don't know yet how to give. This is like an athlete entering a race without knowing how to run. If we haven't learned to give money, we haven't learned anything. Ministry is a life of giving. We give our whole lives; God should have ownership of everything. Remember, whatever we give God control of He can multiply and bless. God's blessing is not so we can amass goods, but so we can be more involved in His enterprise.

Whatever I need to give, God inevitably first calls me to give out of my scarcity—whether I lack money, love, hospitality or information. Whatever God wants to give through us He first has to do to us. We are to partake of the fruit, but we are not to eat the seed. We are to sow it or give it away.

As we experience these phases of worship, we experience intimacy with God, the highest and most fulfilling calling men and women may know. In his book *The Pleasures of God*, John Piper writes, "When we are most satisfied in Him ... we will be most satisfied in God when we know why God Himself is most satisfied in God.

MERCY/VINEYARD

by Christy Wimber

John really was a brilliant businessman and when worship songs started flowing from the Vineyard (which at the time were mostly all John's songs), he began the copyrighting entity "Mercy/Vineyard." At this time most of us kids [John's kids and daughter-in-laws] at some point all worked at Vineyard Ministries International (VMI). One of the areas some of us worked in was song submission (we listened and reviewed incoming worship songs). In fact, we worked many different jobs to earn enough money. John always wanted to make sure we had enough.

But Mercy/Vineyard obviously grew as new worship leaders and new churches were planted through the years. At one point, John began to see a possible way for people to misunderstand him or the worship that was being released. Therefore, he felt it would be wise to make a change. He gave Mercy/Vineyard over to VMI and then over to Vineyard Music.

John did his usual "gathering of the family" (which he didn't really have to do), but he explained everything and we all agreed it was the right thing. This is definitely one of the values I hope to pass on to my kids—that they are part of the ministry we do. John never made anyone, no matter how crazy, young, or loud they were; he never made anyone feel like they were an outsider. And looking back at this family meeting, I don't think any of us really understood how important that decision really was; at least I sure didn't. I was just a kid! John always knew better most of the time. At the time, I don't think any of us saw how important this was, at least I sure didn't. I now see how important that decision probably was. And John didn't want anyone or anything to "taint" the worship God was allowing the Vineyard to be a part of. Honestly, John would say, "If you don't understand what money is for, you don't understand the ministry."

In the coming years obviously we saw an explosion in the Vineyard, and worship had a major role in all of that. Therefore, I think it is most appropriate to add the following excerpt from an interview John did with the Worship Together label/ministry back in the 1990s. Although its immediate context was the worship-driven revival taking place in the U.K. at that time, the content I believe still applies for today.

It is amazing to reflect on how God allowed the Vineyard, through John's leadership, to impact the world in the area of worship. John really understood what and who worship was for. I think God chooses to use and trust people with callings when those involved don't feel the need to make it about themselves or "their ministry." John just happened to be one of those people. In fact, he didn't talk a lot about this song or that CD being released, but more to the writers and worship leaders about their family life, asking often how their kids were doing. One of the last things he ever said to a group of Vineyard songwriters was, "I don't care if you never write another song; what I care about is seeing you in twenty years, married to the same person."

I remember many times when a song that you knew was God-inspired came around; John would get a grin on his face, and usually say something like "That's the real deal there." In the early 1990s I remember driving home from the cabin in the Arrowhead Mountains, with Sean, John, and Carol. We were listening to a new album Vineyard released with one of the worship leaders from the Las Vegas area. John shared the story of this one lady, who at that moment on the album was singing a song titled, "Restore My Soul."

John and Carol loved that song, and talked about what a precious gift worship really is. That is the real deal. And John loved it. He loved it when God would bless us with more stuff to worship Him with. The older I get the more I realize what an amazing and rare leader John was. The legacy of a person is not all they accomplish while on the earth, but also if it continues to stand after they are gone. Obviously John's heritage and legacy in worship stands. John taught us how to be worshipers of the King in all we do, and he lived it out before us.

Christy Wimber *is married to Sean, John Wimber's youngest son. Christy has been involved with the Vineyard since the beginning.*

The following is an excerpt from an article entitled, "The Musician in Revival" by Stuart Townsend for *Worship Together* magazine (reprinted with permission).

Q: John, what's your perspective on what's going on at the moment and how it relates to the worshipping life of the church?

John: The two are very closely linked. Historically every revival move of God has produced music. Sometimes the music actually precipitated revival, sometimes it occurred during revival, but it was always present in the aftermath. Often the new songs were very simple in style, and were actually borrowed from contemporary settings—the popular music of the day, if you will. In this context, the contemporary worship that has been produced in the last thirty years of renewal in the U.K. is very significant. In both the mainline and house church streams, God has raised up teachers and leaders who have emphasized the importance of praise and worship, of adoration and intimacy, and this has produced the dividend of hearts ready and receptive to the work of God in the lives of His people. Just as back in California we dig waterways and ditches and allow water to flow through them, so the teaching and leadership of these people has developed a readiness and hunger for the kind of refreshing that has been triggered around at various places.

But I believe the best is yet to come, not only in terms of the recovery and strengthening of the church, but in the expression of that recovery and strengthening through new songs. That's not to say that today's songs are not good: I thank God all the time for the Graham Kendricks, the Noel Richards, the Chris Bowaters and the many others who contribute wonderfully to the refreshing and renewing of the church, as well as our own music at Vineyard. But in the fire of revival, so to speak, the best music is yet to come.

Q: As writers, musicians and worship leaders, then, how should we prepare for what God has in store for us?

John: The difficulty will not be so much in the writing of new and great music; the test will be in the godliness of those that perform and deliver it. In that sense some of our worship community is not well prepared for revival. Many have been allowed into worship leading because of this new emphasis on contemporary groups and music, and the consequent need for their worship skills and musical skills. But little has been said to them about the need for godliness, spirituality and depths of maturity in their individual and family lives. Quite frankly, many of our musicians are just not steeped in a daily spirituality.

We learned a lot from our own experiences of God's initial outpouring in the Vineyard in 1979, and the following years. In that period we had both blessing and destruction. We had people that were just not ready to be used of God in a highly public way, although you would have thought they were from their gifts of teaching, ministry or music: They were very gifted, they just weren't very godly.

Having worked as a pastor for a number of years, my concern in this current wave is that we all get through this thing, with marriages, families and churches intact, so that we can "give a good report to God in that day."

We need to be aware that in times of great blessing, there is also the potential for great testing and trial. This is not the time for 'business as usual': This is the time to get deep into prayer and God's Word, and deal with those cracks and holes in our spiritual lives, to get our lives in order—because with the blessing goes great pressure.

Q: What kind of pressure?

John: Some of the activity that is going on is quite extreme, and it's incredibly easy in these times to become so enamored of some aspect of the outflow of God, that in trying to protect or champion it, you will find yourself out of line with orthodoxy. Down through the history of the church many wonderful things have happened that have produced much fruit. But certain aspects of these things have led people to get out of line with Scripture and the church, simply because of the excitement of the movement and the intensity of the phenomena, often resulting the birth of a cult.

As leaders we need to remain congruent with orthodoxy and

othropraxy, to maintain our focus on the 'main and the plain' in Scripture. I don't have any particular aspects of this current in mind.

Q: So if we want to keep in step with what God's doing, and be available to be used by Him, how can we practically set about it?

John: Over the last six months I've spent time re-reading some of the evangelical classics, like, *A Christian's Secret to a Happy Life*, by Hannah Whitall Smith. I was given a copy the third week after I became a Christian, and it gave me a context for spirituality, and a foundation for trust and obedience of God. Books like those have taught me that seeking God for experiences and gifts is superficial: We are simply called to seek God!

I've preached many times that we are called to a reverential serving of God with our whole heart and being, stressing that if anything except God is your portion in life, I can't guarantee it: I can't guarantee that your children will be happy, or that your spouse will love you forever ... But I can guarantee that if your desire is Jesus, you'll get Jesus, and you can walk with Him all the days of your life.

When I went through cancer a year or so ago, I was astonished when people from my own church asked me, "Weren't you afraid you were going to die?" After about the fifteenth person, I realized I hadn't really taught my congregation the truth of the Word. I had to get to them and say, "In June of 1963 this man died. And everything from that time to this has been Jesus." I'm not trying to hold onto my life: I gave my life up. When I became a Christian, I was a musician with two albums I had produced in the U.S. Top Ten; it was the establishment of my career after thirteen years of hard work. But God spoke to me in the two-line parable of the pearl of great price: "I want it, give it to me." He didn't say, "Give it to me and I will give you a career as a pastor, or music that will go to many nations of the world." He said,

"Give me everything. Liquidate all your assets, and I will give you the pearl."

Now the pearl isn't a new career, or the opportunity to make a name for yourself as a worship writer or leader. It isn't even the ability to sustain yourself in that profession. If your readers' motivation in being involved in their local church worship is to make a full-time career of it, they'll probably be disappointed.

The pearl is Jesus. And if He is their focus, they'll go right through this revival unscathed. Oh, they'll have to face things, but they will come through in a godly fashion, and they will stand unashamed before the Lord, having been used to refresh a nation—and through that nation probably a whole continent.

We've just been doing a church-planting seminar here, and we've worked out that between 4 and 10 percent of the European Community are tied closely to the church. That leaves something in the region of 270 million people who need to be touched by God. And one of the main means in doing that will be through worship and the worshipping community.

But think about it: if worship leads every move of God, as it did in the Old Testament, where do you think the enemy will attack? And do you think he will have mercy and not attack the point of our weakness? If you think that, you don't know anything about him, and you don't know anything about the art of warfare.

So this is not the time for secret sin; this is the time to pay attention, to sober up, to focus on the things of God, to get rooted in the Word of God and in the church community; to give yourself wholeheartedly to God, and deal with any weakness in your armor. If you do that, glorifying God in your personal, private life as well as your public, professional endeavors, your shield may get a little dented, but you'll come through.

Seven

The Already and Not Yet

"TAKE THE BEST AND GO!"

After the Signs, Wonders and Church Growth seminar hosted by Christian Advance Ministries in Auckland in 1986, my husband Lloyd came home announcing that he had cried his way to healing. Having just welcomed our new baby, I was unable to make the meetings with him, but found his stories intriguing and was keen to hear more. Lloyd said, "I saw a fat man in a track suit wander onto the stage and say, 'Come Holy Spirit' ... and He did!"

In our denomination the 1980s, one was encouraged to "dress sharp." It was not unusual early on in our church plant on a Sunday morning for Lloyd to put on his three-piece gray pinstriped suit, complete with a tie, and go to the downstairs level of our then-location rental house to preach.

By 1986, the church had grown substantially; we bought land and built a facility. And yet, Lloyd was actually to the point of wanting to leave pastoral ministry altogether—he was feeling burned out. So to go to a conference and see John Wimber's approach to ministry and the ensuing signs, power and presence of Jesus fill the place with ordered chaos created a massive paradigm shift in the heart and soul of my husband. It felt like he had met his church tribe. The casual dress, the emphasis on being real, the style of the music, the intelligent teaching on the Kingdom of God all had a sense of coming home for him. He continued to tell me stories, "As I sat there in my seat, I felt the Holy Spirit said to me, 'Watch this man, and watch what he does, because one day you will be doing what he does."

Not only was Lloyd impacted by the authentic, "normal" approach to ministry, but he was so excited about the worship. He told me, "As soon as I saw the speaker stacks, the size of the drum kit and heard the guitar distortion, I knew I was home."

Vicki Rankin and her husband Lloyd pastor the Auckland Vineyard and oversee the Vineyard Churches in New Zealand.

———◆———

There are two basic concepts that are very important to understand as believers. The first is to be aware that this world's system is under Satan's control and the second is that Jesus Christ came to change all of Satan's plans. Christ accomplishes this by declaring war. First, we will look at how this world lies in the lap of the enemy.

The apostle John writes:

> *We know that we are children of God, and that the whole world is under the control of the evil one.*
>
> *— 1 John 5:19*

Jesus began changing all of Satan's plans by declaring war. In Luke 4 we see an occasion in which Jesus is in the synagogue. He stands up and reads from a scroll, from Isaiah: "The Spirit of the Lord is upon me because he has anointed me to preach good news to the poor." This is the good news of Jesus that He was proclaiming—that the empowerment of the enemy has been broken and Jesus has come! Jesus continues:

> *He sent me to proclaim freedom to the prisoners and recovery of sight to the blind, to release the oppressed and to proclaim the year of the Lord's favor.*
>
> *— Luke 4:18-19*

In doing so, Jesus was issuing a challenge. By picking up on the providence of God and the prophetic utterance of the prophet of Isaiah and reading it that day in the synagogue, Jesus was announcing His intention. He was declaring war on the enemy and He was making it clear—"This is what I am going to do, and these are the things I am going to accomplish."

We are in a time where Jesus has come and broken the power of the enemy. Jesus has done it by living a sinless, perfect life, dying on the cross and providing access for you and me to have fellowship with the Father. In this process, God has demonstrated His love and power once and for all. God has pulled back the covers on the enemy and shown us his strategies, his wiles, his programs, his teachings, and his limitations of power.

We have been fashioned into a people of God, and as a consequence of this we have authority and empowerment to do the works of the God (see Acts 10:38). We need to know that, as believers, God's power is available. The enemy is still in control to the degree that he hasn't been totally vanquished, but there will be a time when the Lord will appear and it will be accomplished. Between now and then we have been set as a military force to engage the enemy and to conquer him in the arenas God is directing us in. We are in a time where Jesus has come and broken the power of the enemy. Christ stands victorious over the principalities and powers in His sinless, perfect life, death on the cross and resurrection, providing access for you and me to have a relationship with the Father.

THE SPIRITUAL BATTLE

The Apostle Paul makes much of the fact that Christ is seated "at [the Father's] right hand in the heavenly realms, far above all rule and authority, power and dominion, and every title that can be given, not only in the present age but also in the one to come" (Ephesians 1:20-21).

Christ is now in place of absolute authority over all other authorities; He is "the only ruler, the King of kings and the Lord of lords" (1 Timothy 6:15). Yet there is a tension all Christians feel—evil has not yet been eradicated in this world.

For a time until the day of the Lord has completed at His

return at the consummation of the ages, we must live under two kingdoms: the kingdom of Satan and the Kingdom of God.

In his book *Christ and Time*, Lutheran theologian Oscar Cullmann compares our situation to that of the Allies in World War II after D-Day. The decisive battle of the war was fought and won by the Allies on D-Day, June 6, 1944. However, the war continued and was not over until months later! More American lives were lost between D-Day and V-E Day than at any other time during the war. So it is with Jesus; our D-Day is Easter Sunday, and our V-E Day is the second coming. Between the two, the war wages on.

How do we know the will of our Father so we may cooperate with His work here on earth? We are in war, and in war there are many battles, like those the Allies faced in World War II, but we will win most of them. The Kingdom of God comes intermittently, according to Father's will, and that is why it is our job to find out what His will is and cooperate with Him here on earth. He has a strategy, though we may not always (if ever) discern it. Our part is to pray, *Your kingdom come, Your will be done on earth as it is in heaven*, then trust and obey. If we die trusting God, then our death contributes to fulfilling His purposes.

> **If we die trusting God, then our death contributes to fulfilling His purposes.**

The Kingdom is both future and present, it has been fulfilled in Christ's first coming and will be consummated in his second coming. To quote George Eldon Ladd, we live between the "already and the not yet," between the cross' victory over sin and Satan and the coming age inaugurated by Christ's return.

We have the assurance of eternal life now, and we experience the benefits of the Kingdom only in part. The 16th-century reformer John Calvin put it this way in his "Sermons on Ephesians":

We must endure patiently, because God will not have us come to His kingdom with, so to speak, one leap, but will have us negotiate this world through thorns and briars, so that we shall have much trouble in getting through and we shall be in great distress. Seeing that He will have us led by such a way, and yet nevertheless gives us so good a remedy as ought to be sufficient for us—which is that He strengthens us with invincible constancy by His Holy Spirit—let us stand ready to fight till the time of victory is fully come.

That is why Paul prays that we may know the "incomparably great power" that raised Jesus from the dead and seated Him in heavenly places. He prays that we might be equipped with Kingdom power because for a time we must do battle in an evil world.

I pray that your eyes may be enlightened in order that you may know the hope to which he has called you, the riches of his glorious inheritance in the saints, and his incomparably great power for us who believe. That power is like the working of his mighty strength.

– Ephesians 1:18-19

THE CHRISTIAN LIFE AS WARFARE

The Crimean War of 1853-1856 pitted Russia against England and France fighting over a peninsula in the Black Sea. The war is probably best known for the disastrous charge of the Light Brigade. At the battle of Balaclava, the British were picture perfect as they advanced on the Russian guns, oblivious to the deadly fire from all sides. No cavalry attack was ever executed with such precision, discipline, and bravery. Yet as a French general watched his doomed allies advance, he remarked, "It's magnificent, but it's not war."

In the nearly 2,000 years since Jesus Christ commissioned His disciples to go into all the world and make disciples, the Church has made its mark on civilization. Empires have risen. Lands have been conquered. Great works of art have been created. Libraries full of theological and philosophical arguments have been erected, all in the name of Christ. The cultural legacy of Christianity has truly been magnificent.

But it's not war, and the Christian life is warfare. The Church is called to be a family, a hospital, a school and an army. The Church had better be an army because, whether we realize it or not, we're in the middle of a war. A war between the Kingdom of God and the kingdom of Satan.

Matthew 28:18-20 gives us the big picture. Jesus Christ, resurrected, gives His marching orders to His disciples:

> *Jesus came to them and said, "All authority in heaven and on earth has been given to me. Therefore, go and make disciples of all nations, baptizing them in the name of the Father, and of the Son and of the Holy Spirit, and teaching them to obey everything I have commanded you. And surely, I am with you until the end of the age."*

We see the commanding officer—Jesus the Christ—with all authority in heaven and earth. We have the army—Jesus' disciples. We have the mission—go and make disciples of all nations. And we see the nucleus of the conflict—teaching men and women to obey the commandments of Jesus.

When the Church carries out these specific orders, the result is warfare. Neglecting this duty may be worthwhile in a temporal sense, but it's not the war. And war is our destiny as the Church.

SPIRITUAL WARFARE: OUR ENEMY

Warfare implies an enemy. When World War I broke out, the

war ministry in London dispatched a coded message to one of the British outposts in an inaccessible area of Africa. The message read: "War declared. Arrest all enemy aliens in your district."

The War Ministry received this prompt reply: "Have arrested ten Germans, six Belgians, four Frenchmen, two Italians, three Austrians, and an American. Please advise immediately who we're at war with."

The situation seems ludicrous. How can you fight a war unless there's agreement about who the enemy is? As Christians we are in a declared war, but unless we're clear about whom the enemy is, we'll waste our time fighting enemies who aren't enemies at all.

A reading of the New Testament leaves little doubt about who the enemy is: "Be self-controlled and alert. Your enemy the devil prowls around like a roaring lion looking for someone to devour" (1 Peter 5:8).

In his book *The Christian Warfare*, Martin Lloyd-Jones reminds us that we can only understand the contemporary world in terms of the unusual activity of the devil and the "principalities and powers" of darkness:

> Indeed, I suggest that belief in a personal devil and demon activities is the touchstone by which one can most easily test any profession of Christian faith today. In a world of collapsing institutions, moral chaos, and increasing violence, never was it more important to trace the hand of "the prince of the power of the air." If we cannot discern the chief cause of our ills, how can we hope to cure them?

It's hard enough resisting the real enemy. That's a full-time job. If we start fighting other Christians, we're fighting two wars, and one of them is suicidal. Someone once said that "the Christian church is the only army that shoots its wounded." Not only do we shoot our wounded but much of the time the generals are taking target practice at each other.

The apostle Paul's letter to the Ephesians would be such a lovely book if it stopped around the end of the fifth chapter. We could rejoice in the fact that Christ reigns as head over all. We could be in awe of the sublime truth that the Church is one body, one family, and one holy temple. We could be inspired as the Church to learn to live as a body, a family, and a holy temple.

But that's not the whole picture. Fortunately for us Paul also includes the gritty reality of the Christian life. The glorious work of God in Christ that Paul discusses in Chapters 1-5 of Ephesians is under attack. The enemy of every Christian—Satan, or the devil—is constantly hatching schemes to undo God's work. Satan cannot even begin to harm God, so he seeks to bring harm to what God values. That's why we have Ephesians 6. It's a warning.

Paul continues by cataloging the different components of the armor of God. He talks about how to put it on and how to use it. We see both offensive weaponry and protective armament. We usually individualize our understanding of warfare. But remember, soldiers don't go into battle alone; they go in as an army.

The armor of God is not only for the benefit of the individual, but also for all of Christ's community. As individuals we put on the armor because we need to be vigilant against Satan's attack on the whole Church.

SPIRITUAL WARFARE: PROCLAMATION

Ephesians 6 is often viewed in individual terms; that is, each individual Christian should pray and ask God for strength to do battle. Paul actually depicted the armor in corporate terms. The whole Church is involved in the process of arming. In fact, each believer is responsible for arming other believers.

In the war we fight, the objective isn't geo-political. The territory we try to gain control of is not measured by political boundaries; the body of Christ knows no nationalistic agenda. Our country is measured by the landscape of the human heart. When a person believes in Jesus Christ, he or she becomes a child of God, and one more soul is transferred from the kingdom of darkness to the kingdom of light.

Satan's kingdom is assaulted today in the same way he was in the New Testament, through the words and works of Jesus.

According to Paul, the primary aggressive action the Christian is called to take in the world is to spread the gospel—the good news of salvation through the death and resurrection of Christ. The Gospel represents God's power to rescue people from the devil's tyranny.

Thus the traditional imagery of warfare is turned on its ear. As Jesus commands, we don't "live by the sword." We approach this warfare not as a spiritual Rambo ready to blow away anything that moves, but more as an ambassador, who is also working behind the scenes to free spiritual hostages:

> *And the Lord's servant must not quarrel; instead, he must be kind to everyone, able to teach, not resentful. Those who oppose him he must gently instruct, in the hope that God will grant them repentance leading them to a knowledge of the truth, and that they will come to their senses and escape from the trap of the devil, who has taken them captive to do his will.*
>
> *– 2 Timothy 2:24-26*

A GOOD SOLDIER MUST LOOK CAREFULLY

Fighting a war isn't as easy as listening to the latest conference CD or attending a two-day seminar; discerning, confronting, and overcoming the enemy of our souls isn't as simple as we would like. Before grabbing an unfamiliar weapon and heading out into the front lines, a soldier must take a careful look at the history of the conflict he is enlisted to fight. He will want to discover all he can about the larger issues at stake, the actual battleground, the enemy's plans and patterns of attack, the strategies proven effective in past battles, and the scope of his own mission.

Let's be good soldiers and do some biblical investigation before we go out in search of the latest "technology" in spiritual warfare.

KINGDOMS AT WAR

Previously I mentioned that we are indeed engaged in is a conflict between two kingdoms—God's Kingdom and Satan's kingdom. Spiritual warfare is kingdom warfare. To whatever extent we participate in this war, the conflict encompasses much more than our individual temptations, struggles and sicknesses, setbacks and breakthroughs. Two vast armies are arrayed against each other in an ongoing battle that has spanned nations and generations since the dawn of time.

God and all who serve him comprise the kingdom of light. God's Kingdom is an eternal kingdom powerfully advancing in the world today. Opposing God on the battlefield of human history is Satan and all whom he has deceived and enslaved to do his bidding. This kingdom of darkness is retreating before the light of God's sovereign purposes, yet it remains a powerful threat to all who are godly and all that is good. Much of the conflict is unseen as the devil challenges God's right to rule, demons contest the assignments given angels, and both angelic ministers and demonic minions carry our their respective masters directives in the world of men.

But the conflict is not entirely invisible. We witness Kingdom warfare in the lives of men and women who turn from a life of sin to trust God and obey His Word. Kingdom conflict is apparent in the breakdown of marriages and families, as well as in the recovery of addicts and the restoration of broken homes.

We see flashes of Kingdom power as we proclaim the Gospel to the lost, feed the poor, heal the sick, strengthen the church with spiritual gifts, and cast our demons. Kingdom warfare is even evident in the rise and fall of governments, upheaval in social institutions, and economic crises.

> We witness Kingdom warfare in the lives of men and women who turn from a life of sin to trust God and obey His Word.

Two thousand years ago Jesus came to earth to declare a new day. Renewing the message John the Baptist had announced, Jesus inaugurated His ministry by lifting up His voice in Galilee and crying out, "The time has come, the Kingdom of God is near, repent and believe the good news."

This preaching of a kingdom that had now come to earth was much more than a theological reference point for Israel's religious teachers; it was a dramatic war cry, an announcement of imminent confrontation and conflict! The King of kings and Lord of lords had come to challenge the prince of this world. To understand the excitement that this announcement stirred wherever Jesus went, we have to glance back at the Old Testament's revelation of God's sovereignty and the promise of a coming king.

THE ANTICIPATION OF THE KINGDOM

In the clearest language, the Old Testament declares the God of the Bible to be heaven's High King, the Almighty God, the Sovereign Ruler of the universe. He is the eternal creator of all that exists, the initiator and finisher of all things. He sits in heaven, enthroned in majesty and power, surrounded by angels who carry out His will. If we could see God as he is right now, our breath would be taken away by the scene the prophet Isaiah glimpsed (see Isaiah 6:1-6) or John described (see Revelation 4). Our knees would buckle and our hearts would pound with the pulse of the ancient Psalm:

> *The Lord is the great God, the great King above all gods. In his hand are the depths of the earth and the mountain peaks belong to him. The sea is his for he made it, and his hands formed the dry land. Come let us bow in worship, let us kneel before the Lord our Maker.*
>
> *– Psalm 95:3-6*

When we read of this King's kingdom, the central meaning of the Old Testament term for kingdom is dynamic. That is, God's kingdom is not a localized place or a distinctive people group, though He rules over places and people. Rather, God's kingdom is His reign, His rule, His dominion, His power and authority in action, bringing all things into alignment with His sovereign will.

God's Kingdom is His reign, His rule, His dominion, His power and authority in action.

God's Kingdom is His dynamic reign and rule—and nowhere is this clearer than in the poetic parallelism of the Psalms wherein God's Kingdom is revealed to be synonymous with His might, His dominion, and His throne.

Against heaven's King and His absolute right to rule, Satan, our adversary, rebelled and led a heavenly revolt. Coming to earth, the Evil One seduced humanity's parents with lies that tempted them to distrust God and embrace a life of independence. The consequence of Adam and Eve's sin is a tired old story. Created to love God and enjoy one another in a relationship of trust and freedom, they were abruptly introduced to the ravages of fear and painful isolation. The clear light of trust and transparency in all their relationships was overshadowed by the oppressive darkness of shame and suspicion. Freedom and fellowship with God were exchanged for bondage and alienation. From the earliest pages of Genesis this was to become the story of mankind—our story.

Life is hard. No, it's worse than that—life can be hell. Our own flesh—our humanity—has been infected by sin, producing irrational thinking and erratic, self-destructive behavior. Sickness, disease, and death continually threaten us. False teachers and empty philosophies deceive many. Storms, famines, floods, and earthquakes ravage the earth. The world system of political, social, and economic relationships has become cruel and oppressive. And, a demonic host of unseen adversaries tempt, torment, attack, and enslave all who are most vulnerable. All of the evils that men suffer and commit against each other in alienation from God are manifestations of Stan's tyrannical rule—his own kingdom of darkness.

Through the unfolding drama of the Old Testament, God responded to mankind's terrible predicament by calling and raising up various individuals and groups to be a blessing in the earth, to break the power of darkness, to establish righteousness, and to renew worship of the one true God.

Think of how God worked so powerfully through Noah and Abraham, David and Solomon, Samuel and Elijah. Nowhere is the power of God's Kingdom more clearly manifest in the Old Testament that in the life of Moses, the plagues upon Egypt, and the exodus of God's people from captivity. Through all of Israel's patriarchs, judges, kings, prophets, and priests, God repeatedly called people to repent and to return to Him.

If they would trust Him and once again walk in His ways, God promised to rescue them and make them a blessing to the nations.

But through the generations of the Old Testament, God promised that a day would come when He would visit the earth in power and majesty to break the bonds of wickedness and oppression, to redeem mankind from its slavery, and to reestablish His own Kingdom of righteousness and peace. No longer would He raise up human representatives to cry out against wickedness and evil; but in a future day, *He* would come in power and might to set life in order.

Yes, God is King in heaven, but He promised His people that He would someday come down to earth and make His sovereignty manifest among men and nations. This present evil age would finally give way to the new and glorious age to come.

The Old Testament prophets trembled with this hope:

> *Oh, that you would rend the heavens and come down, that the mountains would tremble before you!*
>
> *– Isaiah 64:1*

Generations of faithful men and women like Simeon and Anna prayed and waited for coming of that day often called, "The Day of the Lord." The Old Testament era drew to a close with a great sense of expectation. Isaiah and Daniel had foreseen a vast and majestic heavenly Kingdom coming to earth. Malachi prophesied the return of Elijah at the dawn of that great day.

EXPECT SOME RESISTANCE

In any battle there are going to be casualties. Although ultimately Jesus Christ has already won the war, that doesn't mean there aren't going to be setbacks and skirmishes. We are to suffer some losses. Wherever there is a church obeying the words and doing the works of Jesus, there is an outpost of the Kingdom of God. And the outpost is always in the middle of hostile territory.

Count on it: Any turf you win, you're going to have to defend. The enemy doesn't just say, "Oh well, I guess we'll have to leave because the Christians are getting their act together." No. The forces of evil may fall back, but they won't permanently retreat.

Years ago we had approximately eight Vineyard churches in the Los Angeles area. We then suffered a ferocious attack by the enemy, and most of those churches have since closed down. In New York City, we planted six churches before we got one that lived.

Now think about that. If you were a young couple and you have five babies that died before you got one that lived, you would know the heartbreak. And that's exactly the heartbreak of God when we plant these communities and they don't survive. What's our response? Let's refine our strategy, hone our training, and plant more. Let's just plant twice as many this time. And keep planting until we've reached all the lost and people have found authentic community in Christ.

There's a point in spiritual warfare where you decide you won't be beaten. You're going to keep going until Jesus returns. I cannot tell you how many times I've gone to sleep saying, "God, I'm not going to quit no matter how bad I feel. No matter what they do, no matter what happens next."

Paul exhorted Timothy to "endure hardship with us like a good soldier of Jesus Christ" (2 Timothy 2:3). A soldier's life includes hardship. A good soldier endures it without giving up.

SPIRITUAL WARFARE: TRIUMPH

As a biblically-rooted Christian, I always formally believed in the devil. This only became real, however, when I prayed one night for a friend's deliverance from his cocaine addiction. Several demons noisily departed, and in the morning his obsession with drugs was gone for the first time in years. His healing had begun!

Despite such "power encounters," it is as futile to talk about the devil to the secular mind as it is to talk about light to a bat. The Bible reveals and then simply assumes Satan's fallen activity, ravaging the planet out of pure hatred for God. As Israel battled the pagan nations, she also battled the dark powers behind their idols. Jesus forced the enemy into the open, driving out his demons from the oppressed. The devil then bloodied the early church and left his mark of death and deception on the Christian centuries to follow.

For Martin Luther, the Reformation was a spiritual battle. He fought Satan, targeting him with an inkwell and holding up the cross before him. Not believing in the devil is like not believing in smog; while you don't see it, it's in the air you breathe, polluting your lungs as a result. The madness of our modern age hasn't come out of some black hole in outer space.

As a young man, Karl Marx made his own personal pact with a cultic group. After World War II Albert Speer, Hitler's architect, reflected, "It's hard to recognize the devil when he has his hand upon your shoulder."

Seeing with new eyes, we can now understand Paul's triumphant announcement that Christ has "disarmed" the demons, these supernatural "powers and authorities," making a public spectacle of them" by marching them in His victory parade, "triumphing over them by the cross."

But how were these powers armed originally? How have they been disarmed? And how can we stay free from them?

VICTORY AT THE CROSS

Paul writes, "Having disarmed the powers and authorities, He [Christ] made a public spectacle of them, triumphing over them by the cross" (Colossians 2:15). In what way did Jesus accomplish this? How did He disarm the powers and authorities when they're apparently still in place and still able to do some dreadful harm to the uninitiated? Jesus did so by showing us the way out. This way exists in two senses:

Initially, Christ shows us that in Him there is protection, safety, security, identity, and salvation. In Christ, there is salvation, justification, sanctification, and glorification. The whole continuum of the work of God is in Christ, and therefore in us (see Galatians 2:20 and John 17). Because we're in Christ and Christ is in us, we live in the very presence of the Father Himself. Jesus ushers us in to a higher dimension of life, and all of the work of salvation is on Him. Jesus demonstrated this for us, and He demonstrated this to the principalities and powers that be—the world-system and satanic forces. He disarmed the powers and authorities by arming us with the knowledge and reality of our lives as children of God.

> We are taking someone out of the kingdom of darkness and bringing them into the kingdom of light.

Further, Christ trains us by example on how to do spiritual warfare. In the early days some young people would ask me, "Aren't you scared of demons?" And I would say, "No, I'm more scared of God than I am of demons."

You see, I really believe that we have been called into warfare. My commander-in-chief says, "Do war." I think it's best that I do what my Lord has asked me to do. Jesus has unveiled His strategic directives to those who have eyes to see and ears to hear; within the whole spectrum of society there are people who know the imprint, activity, strategies, and limitations of the principalities and powers of Satan. We, the people of God, are to be so attuned. We have been given marching orders.

The apostle John testifies that Jesus "came to tear down the work of the enemy" (1 John 3:8). This is what we do every time we cast out a demon, heal the sick, struggle on behalf of the poor, or lead someone to Christ.

Every time we train up a disciple, every time we teach someone to walk in the guidance and council of God, we are tearing down the enemy's work. We are taking someone out of the kingdom of darkness and bringing them into the kingdom of light.

BAPTISM AS A DEDICATION

Mark is an account of the "good news" that is steeped in military understandings. The very first sentence of the book reads, "The beginning of the Gospel about Jesus Christ, the Son of God ..." Who? The Son of God is the declaration. Mark wants no confusion and no hesitancy in understanding: He is giving an account of the Son of God! This declaration concerning Him and the fact of His coming was so powerful that it changed the course of redemptive history for all eternity, establishing the work of Jesus Christ, His ministry, and His cross. It gave provision for all of those who heard the Gospel from that day forward, receiving it in trust and entering into it as a way out of the predicament of the darkness they were born into.

As I said, battle imagery permeates this writing. In Mark 1:9 we see that Jesus came from Nazareth of Galilee and was baptized by John in the Jordan River. Now, we wouldn't normally think of baptism as an act of war, but it is. We tend to think of baptism in sentimental, nostalgic language, particularly if we are thinking of infant baptism or as a rite or ceremony to join a church.

But when you see it as an act of obedience and testimony, it is a declaration of war. When you go under that water, according to Romans 9, you go under as a dead person, being buried there and you're brought forth in resurrection as a new creation. And when you're coming up out of that water, what you are saying to the world is that now you stand for Jesus Christ. I've chosen Jesus and I will stand with Jesus from this day forward. This is an act of warfare.

Jesus did not get baptized for remission of sin. In fact, when Jesus asked His cousin John to baptize Him, John says to Jesus that He should be baptizing him. He knew that Jesus was sinless. But Jesus insists, so that "all righteousness will be fulfilled." Jesus saw in the provision of baptism something that He wanted to identify with, so that His called-out ones—the Church—would do the same from that day forward.

Jesus saw a declaration, a dedication of Himself to the Father that could only be accomplished through the initiation of baptism. Baptism was a provision of God that demonstrated identification and commitment to purity of life and a new order of existence. Immediately after Jesus gets baptized, He also gets tested:

> *At that time Jesus came from Nazareth in Galilee and was baptized by John in the Jordan. As Jesus was coming up out of the water, He saw heaven being torn open and the Spirit descending on Him like a dove. And a voice came from heaven: "You are my Son, whom I love; with you I am well pleased." At once the Spirit sent Him out into the desert, and He was in the desert forty days, being tempted by Satan. He was with the wild animals, and angels attended Him.*
>
> *– Mark 1:9-13*

In other words, warfare begins immediately. He identifies with the Father, embracing His Father's love and acceptance, and immediately He's thrown into warfare.

AGENTS OF DELIVERANCE

One of the tasks we have as believers is "deliverance." Luke 11 contains the story where Jesus is being accused of evil activities

and identified with the demon Beelzebub. In the midst of this
exchange, Jesus says:

> *When an evil spirit comes out of a man it goes through an*
> *arid of places seeking and rest and does not find it. Then it*
> *says, I will return to the house I left and when it arrives it*
> *finds the house swept clean and put in order. Then it goes*
> *and takes seven other spirits more wicked than itself, and*
> *they go in and live there. And the final condition of the man*
> *is worse than the first.*
>
> *– Luke 11:24-26*

Here the Scripture is speaking of a deliverance that has taken
place and the "house" is clean. At this point in time it needs to be
furnished appropriately. When we pray for people and minister
deliverance to them, the first thing we do is find out if they are
Christians. If they aren't, then we need to lead them to Christ and
at that point they need to be filled with the Holy Spirit. If they
are Christians and somehow have fallen into sin, then we deal
with that—we invite them to confess their sin and get rid of very
vestige of demonic influence. Then we give instruction on how
demons can come back and attack them again.

In the early days of the Vineyard we didn't realize the importance of all the instruction and empowerment. We did not spend
enough post-operative time with those we took through deliverance. We did not realize that the demons could come back so
readily. But they often did; it was pitiful and a shame.

As we caught on, we did a better job serving and empowering
these people. Today I hope we are doing a good job all the time
because we now know that we have the authority over Satan and
his demons. The more you "do the stuff" that Jesus did, the more
you learn.

CAN DEMONS COME BACK?

I think it is very important to understand this: If you have ever been delivered from a demon you can count on them coming back. This is their job, and they are persistent. They will come back in attempt to regain and recoup any ground that they have lost by losing you as a vehicle to carry out their plans.

It's very important that you understand your authority as a believer in Jesus Christ. Take the time to know who you really are, what empowerment is and the tools you have in Christ that will keep you protected. I don't write this to scare you, but to remind you that you are in a war and you need to be aware and on guard against the enemy and his schemes.

In John 5 we read the story of healing at the pool of Bethesda. Jesus enters the pool area and He sees a man who had been crippled for 38 years. Jesus asks the man if he wants to be made whole, and the man begins whining bout how he is unable to get into the water there, which was reputed to have healing properties.

The man said he had tried many times to get someone to help him, but no one would, and in the midst of the man whining to Jesus, Jesus says, "Rise, take up your bed and be made whole." The man did exactly what Jesus said and was completely healed!

A big commotion follows and Jesus disappears. Later when Jesus finds the man and begins to dialogue with him, Jesus says, "Go and sin no more lest a worst thing befall thee." Jesus' words indicate, in this particular case, that this man's paralysis was directly related to sin and if he went back to the sin that had caused the paralysis he would be in a worse state.

Is all sickness caused by sin? I believe that the answer to that is no. Not everyone is sick due to sin they have committed or that which has been committed against them. But in a general way, we wouldn't have any sickness in the world if there hadn't been any sin. Adam and Eve were not created to be sick beings. They would have had divine health, but because of their sin, consequences—including pain and sickness and ultimately death—have entered into the world (see Genesis 3:14-19).

It is the agenda of demons to come back again and again to gain any ground that they may have lost after being cast out. In knowing this, remember to remain alert and not to give the enemy any way in. Know your weaknesses, especially if you have been healed or delivered. Christ has set you free. Do not choose to go back to any lifestyle or pattern of sin that can open yourself up to demonic activity once again (see John 5:14).

Getting free and staying free are both key. It is important to know what you have weakness towards and keep yourself in a place where accountability is present. In a community environment, keep clean and continue getting prayer.

THE POWER OF DECEPTION

Because we are free from the actual bondage of sin, deception is one of the chief ways the enemy works in our lives. It's important that as believers we know truth; Jesus is truth and there is no deception in Him. Many of us get victimized from time to time because we believe a lie. Even as children of light, the enemy can have power anytime we accept a lie.

The enemy is full of lies, and often times the enemy whispers to us thoughts about ourselves, even in the "first person" voice. It may be a lie about us—something that accuses or condemns us. It could be a lie that another person has spoken over us. If we give in and accept this lie, the enemy can come in and beat our ears down!

Maybe when you were a child an adult said to you, "You're a thief and you always will be!" And here you are 35 years old and maybe you haven't stolen anything in years but that saying replays over and over in your mind: I know I'm a thief because Uncle Charlie said I would be. It altered your inner perception of yourself and the enemy has found a foothold, a place in you.

And so an opportunity arises to take a little something and the seeming need for theft arises. So, you comply and the enemy says, "See! I told you that you were a thief!"

But if you're sensitive to the stirring of the Holy Spirit within you, something will well up and say, "Wait a minute! I'm a new person, I came to the cross, my identity is now in Christ and all things have been made new. I'm free from the neediness of the past, and I'm not a thief, I'm a giver."

Take the lie to the cross and leave it there; don't let the enemy bring the old you out and deceive you by saying, "This is just the way you are." Give it to Christ, and remember who you are in Christ. Then relinquish your false identity. Go and steal no more.

So many times we get bogged down with past sins and past words spoken against us. The only path to freedom is by taking it to the cross and not giving in to the lies of the enemy. God has forgotten our sin altogether (see Hebrews 10:17). The enemy will continue to attack us; we just have to remember that and stay in the battle. The war doesn't stop because we need it to stop; it goes on; therefore, we must go on fighting.

ATTACK COUNTER-ATTACK

All through Scripture there is continual interaction of attack and counterattack. Another word for attack we can use is "fronts," thinking in terms of warfare. I myself am a World War II kid. I can remember laying on the floor with a world map imagining where my relatives were—my mother had several brothers and many of my cousins were in different parts of the United States Army, Navy and Marine Corps.

Some fought in the East, some fought at Guadalcanal, and some fought in the Pacific and Africa. Others eventually went into the main part of Europe and fought up through Italy. I can clearly remember in 1944 listening to the radio and following all the different battles that were going on. A war is not a battle; a war is made of many battles that come and go. Similarly in the Christian dynamic of life, you'll fight many battles in your lifetime, but the war is already won.

In this case there's no question of the outcome. Jesus won the war at the cross, but in the interim time, you and I have work to do. We have been assigned the task of doing the mop-up work, the clean-up work of ridding the world of the foul presence of the enemy. We are the people of God, and we have the Holy Spirit within us, upon us, and behind us, leading and directing us into the conflict and the work that we do. But we are also dealing with people who are impregnated, as it were, with spiritual power—the power of darkness. The inevitable result is attack and counter-attack.

> **We are the people of God, and we have the Holy Spirit within us, upon us, and behind us, leading and directing us into the conflict and the work that we do.**

These attacks are violent at times. There's violence in the Kingdom of God. Coming to Christ is not a matter of simply coming to Jesus and expecting all your problems to be over. In fact, nothing could be further from the truth. You may not have the problems you once had before you were saved, but you still have problems. I haven't had a hangover for over 30 years because I have a new identity, but now I have a completely different set of problems!

In the old days, under the dominion of darkness, my problems were my behavior, the things I did. My behavior is still an issue, but now it's more attitudinal than action-oriented. The things I used to do were an embarrassment and shameful to me. Once in awhile I will feel that same shame when my attitude doesn't line up with Jesus; when this happens I repent once again. The Lord has ways of dealing with our attitude.

Every advance in the Kingdom, whether in character or in the exercise of faith, will be met with a counterattack. I taught about healing in almost every sermon for close to a year, even though we didn't see any healings for close to nine months. In fact, two or three people died. Some even left our church because they thought I was teaching the heresy of divine healing. At times I wondered if I was crazy to keep teaching on the subject with no visible benefit to the congregation. This was a test. I asked myself, "Can I continue to believe and practice what the Scriptures teach regardless of the results?" I had to answer, "Yes." I had learned that being embarrassed was not sufficient reason for abandoning obedience to the Lord.

So we continued to pray for the sick in compliance with the Word. Once again, I felt humbled by obeying the biblical principle to pray for the sick with no particular guarantee that the Lord would ratify it. I had to prepare myself to continue to act on what I believed the Scriptures taught even if it meant we saw no immediate results. The Lord taught me perseverance during this time.

Whether it is prayer for the sick or a devotional Bible study, when we make commitments to the Lord to act on our beliefs, we can expect the enemy to challenge them. What happens when you decide to start a spiritual discipline such as reading your Bible daily? All hell breaks loose when you begin! The enemy will supply you with a million reasons not to do it. That's his job, and you have to admit he's pretty good at it. But if you will accept that challenge, and go forward anyway, you'll find that you're progressing with more and more insight. From there you will continue to gain momentum and skill. The enemy of our souls will challenge our commitment; perseverance produces growth.

NO HOLD ON ME

You may not have realized what you signed up for when you made a stand for Jesus Christ? I realized early on as a pastor that many people were not aware of what they were entering. The enemy wants the Church wiped out, and do you know why? It's not because we're so significant in and of ourselves; we're just people, the people of God. But that's just what the enemy doesn't like. It's being people of God that makes the difference. We're God's called-out ones; He builds His Church.

When Jesus is taken into the desert to be tempted, the Holy Spirit led Him for forty days. In Luke 4 the Greek word *peirazo* that is translated "temptation" is also easily translated into the word "attack." Attack-temptation is a continuum. It doesn't really matter how the enemy tries to distract you as long as he can get you out of place. If he can do it with enticement, he'll do that; if he can do it by making you sick, he'll do that; if he can get you angry and bitter that will work too. Whatever it takes to get you to quit operating in the Kingdom of God and cease doing the things God has called you to have accomplished our enemy's end.

In John 14:30, the enemy is coming and Jesus says, "He has no hold on me." No inroads, no handles, nothing to entice you with; no way the enemy could attack. Don't give the enemy any space. Don't give him any way in to your life, and don't let him keep you away from God and the plan that God has for you.

Eight

Power for a Purpose

"DOIN' THE STUFF"

John Wimber was my pastor for 20 years and my boss for 12. I had the privilege of traveling with him in ministry situations as well as seeing him at home. I feel very much like the others at his memorial service; I loved him deeply and felt loved by him. There are several mentoring qualities that John had mastered that I have been able to identify as I've reflected on our relationship.

John really understood the nature of influence. Proximity, frequency of contact or depth of relationship didn't hinder his mentoring style. He would take advantage of every opportunity to encourage another person. Whether it was a lengthy meeting with a group of national leaders or a casual exchange in the hallway after a service, John would exercise influence. He would remind people of the gifts they had or simply thank them for their commitment. Often, John would reference a quote from John Wesley that he had copied down on the inside of his Bible: "Do all the good you can, by all the means you can, in all the ways you can, in all the places you can, at all the times you can, to all the people you can, as long as ever you can." John certainly took the other John's encouragement to heart and exercised positive influence in the lives of people he encountered daily.

Believing in people was another quality that John had that carries with it profound mentoring implications. He not only believed in people, but also genuinely valued the contribution that each one made, no matter how humble it might be. During David Watson's (John's friend and leader from the U.K.) battle with cancer, he flew to the United States to receive intensive prayer from John and other Vineyard leaders. Shortly after he arrived Tim Milner and I showed up at the Wimbers' home to mow the lawn. Almost immediately, Carol came out and told us that David Watson was there for prayer and asked us if we could come in and pray for him. Here was an internationally recognized Christian leader being ministered to by two gardeners because John Wimber believed in people. Young or old, rich or not so rich, he valued what every member of the Body of Christ contributed, and this belief has great benefits in the lives of others.

John was without question a uniquely gifted man, someone who had the ability to mentor many people in many different ways. These qualities in his life should be grasped and sharpened by any Christian leader who has a desire to positively influence others.

Glenn Schroder is a former pastor at the Anaheim Vineyard. He and his wife, Donna, pastor a Vineyard church in Portland, Oregon.

In the Old Testament, the Kingdom of God was related to Jewish messianic expectation. It was connected with Jewish eschatology, their hope for the future. In historic Judaism, the Kingdom of God was understood in a nationalistic sense. The people carried a military hope—geographic and political—that a nationalistic kingdom might once again be established. It would be a future empire just like the rule of King David. The first century Jews were looking for another king like King David, an anointed Messiah to lead them to political power through military might.

When Jesus spoke of the Kingdom of God, most people thought of a literal kingdom led by the Jewish people. John 6:15 clearly supports this: "Jesus, knowing that they intended to come and make Him king by force, withdrew again to a mountain by Himself." This was also the longing of the disciples, even after being with Jesus for years. Acts 1:6 says, "So when they met together, they asked Him, 'Lord, are you at this time going to restore the kingdom to Israel?'"

Jesus was not talking about a temporal, nationalistic kingdom, nor was He speaking solely of a futuristic, pie-in-the-sky heavenly kingdom, as the term Kingdom of God came to mean among scholars in the intertestamental period. He was announcing the fact that He was establishing His rule on this earth. No longer would Satan have complete dominion over the earth and its inhabitants—Jesus had come with one main purpose in mind: to destroy the activity of Satan in the world. Two of the ways Jesus did this was to heal the sick and cast out demons. The battle was fought over the ownership of human beings. We find instances of conflict between Jesus and Satan concerning, hunger (see John 6); natural catastrophes (see Mark 4:35); sickness (see Luke 7:21); and death (see Luke 7:11).

In all these battles, Jesus was, and continues to be, the victor. In Matthew 12:22-31, Jesus makes it clear that the struggle in which He is engaged is not a civil war within a kingdom. It is rather a battle between the Kingdom of God and the kingdom of the devil. The strong man, Satan, is bound so that his house (Satan's kingdom) may be plundered. Satan's power is curbed, but he was not rendered completely powerless (see Matthew 16:23; Mark 8:33; Luke 22:3).

So what does the Kingdom of God look like for believers?

The word "kingdom" is translated from the New Testament Greek word *basileia*, which implies an exercise of kingly rule or reign. This is different than simply establishing a geographic realm in which a king rules. The Kingdom of God should not be envisioned in nationalistic terms. It is not the same thing as, say, the United Kingdom, whose realm encompasses Great Britain, Scotland, Northern Ireland, and Wales.

A day is coming (the "day of the Lord") when all of creation, willingly and unwillingly, will see and acknowledge Jesus' reign. Then it will be said, "The kingdom of the world has become the kingdom of our Lord and of His Christ, and He will reign for ever and ever" (Revelation 11:15).

But until then, during this age, there remains a mixture of good and evil. Christ's Kingdom is present, but it is present in an evil world (Matthew 13:36-43). Satan still reigns as "prince of this world" and "the ruler of the kingdom of the air, the spirit who is now at work in those who are disobedient" (see John 14:30 and Ephesians 2:2).

We're living in between times, as it were, between the inauguration and the consummation of the Kingdom of God. As George Eldon Ladd said, "We live in the presence of the future."

CHRIST'S RULE

Perhaps nothing is more prevalent in the gospels than the concept of the Kingdom of God. For example, in the beginning of the Gospel of Mark we read, after John was put in prison, Jesus went into Galilee, proclaiming the good news of God. "The time has come," He said. "The Kingdom of God is near. Repent and believe the good news!" (Mark 1:14-15). In Matthew 4:23, prior to the beginning of a long teaching session, Matthew summarized Jesus' ministry in Galilee as involving three things: "teaching in their synagogues, preaching the good news of the kingdom, and healing every disease and sickness among the people."

In Matthew 10:7, after Jesus gave the disciples authority to cast out demons and to heal the sick, He instructs them to preach "the Kingdom of heaven is near," then "heal the sick, raise the dead, cleanse those who have leprosy, and drive out demons." The term Kingdom was always on Jesus' tongue.

And Jesus makes it clear that the battle is between the Kingdom of God and the kingdom of darkness. It is quite obvious that cosmic war has been declared. Jesus has come to invade Satan's kingdom and defeat it. Jesus also gave this mission of bringing in the reign of God to the disciples. "When you enter a town and are welcomed, eat what is set before you. Heal the sick who are there and tell them 'the kingdom of God is near you'" (Luke 10:8-9).

It was in His disciples' preaching and miracles that Jesus saw the fall of Satan—that is, Satan's defeat (Luke 10:18). The enemies of the Kingdom of God are not readily apparent. They're not the "obvious" enemies; instead they are spiritual forces. Understanding the discernment we need in battle, is very important.

We find how Paul instructs the entire church in Ephesus:

> *Put on the full armor of God so that you can take your stand against the devil's schemes. For our struggle is not against flesh and blood, but against the rulers, against the authorities, against the powers of this dark world, and against the spiritual forces of evil in the heavenly realms.*
>
> *– Ephesians 6:11-12*

When Jesus left the earth, He told the disciples that they would be empowered to carry on the mission that He had begun. This included, healing the sick (spiritually, physically, and emotionally) and expelling demons. All this takes power, and that's what He promised in Acts 1:8: "But you will receive power when the Holy Spirit comes upon you, and you will be my witnesses in Jerusalem, and in all Judea and Samaria, and to the ends of the earth."

THE CHURCH THAT JESUS BUILDS

G.K. Chesterton once said, "There is nothing more practical than a good idea." Ideas have consequences and I want to share a few that God has led us to pursue. These are seeds we have sown, and are sowing, all over the world. Insofar as the seed is true to God's Word and imbued with the Spirit, I believe the Vineyard will continue to produce the fruit of the Kingdom in the future.

This treatment is not exhaustive and I do not presume these ideas apply universally. They are not even original. When the Vineyard started, we did not jump on the bandwagon of "God's new thing." Instead, we set out to do an ancient thing in a contemporary way: train people to continue the kingdom ministry of Jesus. Tired of my ministry, I was desperate to see His.

Before doing any ministry, Jesus heard the Father say, "You are my Son whom I love; with You I am well pleased." God unzipped the heavenly dimension and the Spirit arrived on and in Jesus, to empower Him (see Luke 3:22). Jesus was full of the Spirit without measure and empowered for a purpose: to proclaim and demonstrate the kingdom.

What exactly is "kingdom ministry"? Luke gives a glimpse into Jesus' own self-perception. At Jesus' coronation address He announced His kingly agenda:

> *The Spirit of the Lord is on me, because He has anointed me to preach good news to the poor. He has sent me to proclaim freedom for the prisoners and recovery of sight for the blind, to release the oppressed, to proclaim the year of the Lord's favor.*
>
> *– Luke 4:18-19*

In the gospels we find Jesus' action plan for Spirit-empowered ministry: Jesus proclaimed the release of the poor and poor in spirit, declared freedom to prisoners both literal and those bound in sin and darkness; He cast out demons, healed the sick, and mentored disciples to do the same.

Jesus proclaimed and demonstrated God's right to rule creation as He destroyed the works of Satan (1 John 3:8). He equipped followers and promised that they too would do what he did because "everyone who is fully trained will be like his teacher" (see Luke 6:40; Matthew 28:16-20; John 14:12-14). I view this process of Kingdom ministry as a continuum.

"What is Jesus' vision today?" is the question many leaders ask. Sometimes I wonder if we have it right. What I encourage in the Vineyard churches is asking Jesus to build His vision and strategy among us. I am trying to keep up with Him and believe and do what His book says. So what is Jesus' vision? The Kingdom of God.

Our primary aim in life is to love and glorify God, participating in the expansion of His Kingdom in relevant ways in the time allotted us. As communities of the King, churches should model what the Kingdom looks like when God has His way with a group of people.

POWER FOR A PURPOSE

In the Vineyard, we place a priority on being empowered by the Holy Spirit. But the Spirit empowers for a purpose—not just an experience. We seek the active presence of the Spirit to continue Jesus' ministry. At times we almost lose the purpose; at times we seem to lose the power. From the beginning we have attempted, however inadequately, to keep these two together.

> **The Spirit empowers for a purpose — not just an experience.**

For example, after a remarkable outpouring of the Spirit on our young church on Mother's Day 1979, approximately 1,700 people came to faith in Christ.

Our passion to imitate the ministry of Jesus in the power of the Spirit remains. This requires that we follow Jesus out of baptismal waters, through our personal deserts, and into the harvest. We want to take the ammunition of balanced evangelical theology with the fire power of mainstream Pentecostal practice, loading and readying the best of both of these worlds to hit the biblical target of making and nurturing disciples.

To continue Jesus' ministry requires that we adopt His lifestyle. Unfortunately, Christians in the West would rather implement programs. We are blind to our mechanistic assumptions when we reduce ministry to reproducible components and try to apply them indiscriminately. There is nothing wrong, for instance, with a tool for witnessing like The Four Spiritual Laws. It helps believers communicate biblical truth. But should we use it every time? No. We must ask what is appropriate in each situation and learn the art of listening, even as Jesus modeled (see John 5:19, 30).

An early slogan we liked in the Vineyard was, "What is the Father doing?" We tried to enter each ministry situation with that question foremost in our minds. Our experiences in spiritual gifts were an attempt to discern what the Father was up to. Whether the situation was evangelism, healing, budgeting for the poor, or sending a couple across country to plant a church, the important thing was to ask the Father what He was doing. To continue to listen is essential because Jesus is still owner-operator of the Church. It is, after all, His ministry and authority, not ours. Our job is to cooperate.

It is the Lord who adds to the church—not men—and He graciously works within our clumsy efforts. Church growth theory and practices, though helpful, only tell us where to prune and what fertilizer to use. In no way do they cause or even explain the miracle of conversion-based growth.

Our job is to keep on track; we don't forge our own road. Our track is, "What is Father doing?" We know what Father is doing because Jesus speaks to His friends. "My sheep listen to my voice" (John 10:27), therefore whoever belongs to God hears what God says.

We don't just decide we will go heal everyone in the hospital one day—we don't decide anything! We only do what the Father shows us to do.

There were times in Jesus' three-year ministry when the Father wasn't doing anything. Remember when Jesus couldn't do any mighty works because of the people's unbelief?

The reason the Son of God appeared was to destroy the devil's work (see 1 John 3:8). So we, in doing the Father's will, are to bring the Kingdom to people. When we take care of the poor, pray for the sick and clothe the naked, we will be sensitive to Father's leading in the midst of these precious people and in His time we will see sight restored to the blind, the lame walk, and the lepers cleansed.

But remember, these "signs" of the Kingdom are not for the purpose of showing that the Kingdom is here. They point to the fact that our compassionate King is here! Our Lord is the one who heals and delivers out of compassion. It is not a P.R. program to establish Jesus as King. He is King, and our King is full of compassion! He fed the 5,000 not to provide a sign, but because they were hungry. He healed the sick not to provide a sign, but to relieve their suffering. God's Kingdom comes to the lost and the broken because He is full of mercy and compassion.

A HOUSE FOR ALL PEOPLE

Jesus said, "I will build my church, and the gates of Hades will not overcome it" (Matthew 16:18). Peter preached, "God says, I will pour out my Spirit on all people" (Acts 2:17). Evidence confirms that Jesus' prophecies are being fulfilled.

Despite darkness, Jesus is building His church; the Spirit is being poured out all over the world. The percentage of earth's population claiming Christ is growing.

Paul said the church reveals something of the nature of God (Ephesians 3:10). God reconciles the many from different cultures into the one body. We will be a catalyst for authentic world peace, where "the leaves of the Tree of Life are for the healing of the nations" (Revelation 22:2). Jesus will build His church from "every people group," to use my friend Donald McGran's favorite phrase (see Revelation 7:9).

Our purpose is to evangelize the lost, enfold them in new churches, equip them to know and exalt Jesus in every area of life, expanding God's Kingdom through continuing God's ministry.

Have you noticed the zeal of converts? They are blind to flaws and see only the beauty of the vision of their leader (whether historic or contemporary) and the truth within the teachings and practices of their group. The natural human tendency is to think that what you commit to is best, and if it nurtures you, then it obviously is the best, right? Groups easily take on a "true church" attitude even if they formally deny it, and begin expending energy defining who is "in and out."

All too often, groups evolve from a loose, casual association to rigid adherence to insight from a set theory. My hope is that the Vineyard remains a Christ-centered group focused on the main teachings of Scripture as we follow Augustine's ancient advice: "In essentials unity, in nonessentials diversity, in all things charity." We are thankful for the ideas God calls us to implement. If they are solid, it is because they are God's and rooted in the solid rock of Scripture and in tune (at least in part) with some of what the Holy Spirit is doing today. And though the Vineyard is a mere thread in the global tapestry of the church, I believe it is a thread of His weaving. May God always empower us to continue Jesus' ministry!

Nine

Power Healing

"FAITH IS SPELLED, R.I.S.K."

Like many others, I had the experience of hearing John on tape for the first time. When I listened, it felt like "someone had been in my room," like my mail was being read, or my heartbeat was being given language. I knew from that day in 1980 that the rest of my life would be involved with John Wimber. When he came to South Africa in 1982, I saw the principles he taught put into practice. That was different than anything I had ever seen before, even in 13 years of praying for the sick in a Pentecostal church. The concepts were transferable, simple and without hype or religious jargon. After having words of knowledge from the platform, he had people minister healing in the seats where the sick people were. I was praying for the Lord to heal a guy's back, and heard John say, "Costa, stop asking. Open your eyes, watch what's happening and tell the back what you want it to do." I felt awkward doing that, but did—and saw an immediate response! That instruction has been a part of my training vocabulary ever since, and I have seen God honor it in a dozen different nations.

I saw the most powerful expressions of John's healing ministry in private one-on-one sessions, praying for individuals before or after conference times. A friend of mine had a one-year-old girl whose tear ducts did not work. The result was dry eyes and frequent eye infections and was in real danger of losing her eyesight. The father was not sure if healing was for today, but came like Nicodemus in the night and asked if John would pray for his girl. John prayed a simple prayer; the baby looked at him, and began to cry, with tears! So did her dad. The dad leads a church that now teaches and practices that spiritual gifts are indeed for today.

Costa Mitchell is a Vineyard Pastor and Leader of the Vineyard churches in South Africa.

One sunny afternoon in June 1964 my three-year-old son, Sean, wandered away from our home in Yorba Linda, California. When my wife, Carol, noticed Sean was missing, she was not too concerned because our neighborhood was quiet and well protected, being surrounded by eucalyptus trees and some of the many orange groves for which our county was named—Orange County. The groves also provided an ideal environment for honeybees. The backyards of most neighborhoods were dotted with white boxes that housed bee colonies and their bountiful honeycombs. However, when Carol went out into the front yard looking for Sean, she heard screams coming from a backyard down the street. As only a mother can discern, Carol knew instantly that Sean was in serious trouble.

She called out for my help, and we darted down the street. Carol and I found Sean walking aimlessly down the hill of a neighbor's backyard, terror stricken and waiving at stinging bees. He had wandered into a neighbor's set of hives, inciting a swarm of bees. We picked Sean up, brushed off the bees, and whisked him away toward home. On the way I could see the ugly red welts forming all over him. My heart was racing as I ran across several yards, through our front door, and into our bedroom, where I laid Sean down on our bed. By now he had become quiet, perhaps because Carol and I were holding him, but more likely because he was in shock. When I took his shirt off I found more ugly red stings. After the initial shock of seeing Sean in such bad condition, I pulled myself together and began praying for his healing.

But how should I pray? I had only recently been warned by a pastor about what he called the dangers of charismatic gifts like healing and speaking in tongues. "They are divisive," he told me. "And the devil counterfeits them. It's best to stay away from them. What you need is sound doctrine, not excesses like these gifts."

What was I to think? I was still a young Christian and did not want to fall into error. But my son's present condition cut through his arguments. I began to pray for Sean's healing, but I did not know how to pray. I was desperately in need of words when I broke out into a language that I did not understand.

My "tongues" were accented by intermittent salvos of "Heal him, Jesus, heal him." The longer I prayed, the more confidence and power welled up within me. I could feel faith for healing (though at that time I did not know what to call it) being released. As I prayed I could see Sean's welts go away. Within five minutes Sean was sleeping peacefully, and I was highly confused about what had happened.

When he was awakened a few hours later, Sean had only one small red bump on his body. He was healed.

INTRODUCTION TO THE HEALING MINISTRY

We in the evangelical church tend to focus on content. That is to say, we believe that people have to have a doctrinal explanation of the meaning of salvation in order to be initiated into salvation. I recognize the importance of the presentation of the *kerygma*, the Gospel message, and I know that ultimately it has to be presented, but I'm not so sure that is always has to be done in the formal way that we have come to believe.

Many people in the New Testament came to relationship with Christ not having much of an explanation at all; for instance, the nobleman whose son was healed. The nobleman went home and found out the child had begun to get healed the very hour that Jesus said he would. Well, what did they believe? I think they made an initial response of belief to God; they believed that Jesus was from and of God. I don't know if they fully understood at that point who Jesus was. It wasn't declared at that point. I would assume that a time would come in which there would have been more information needed.

On one occasion Jesus walked up to the pool at Bethesda, which was kind of a hospital at the time; probably several hundred people were in attendance. He picked one man and healed him. Later in the day, Jesus and this man had gotten back together. There was a more complete revelation of who Jesus was, and the man believed.

Remember the woman at the well? Jesus was having dialogue with her, all on a very natural plane. Suddenly He knows things about her that she recognizes have a prophetic meaning. She goes into town as a witness and explains her encounter with Jesus' power and, as a result of witnessing to it, many came out and were converted.

> **When healing takes place it leads unto something. Jesus not only came to heal physically, but also the heart.**

Now in one sense we can discount the conversions in Jesus' ministry as a model because people at that point couldn't understand who Jesus was and what He had come to do. But in Acts, after Pentecost, we have a more complete declaration of the Gospel of Jesus than we have actually from Jesus Himself, and my study of Acts has impressed me with how often something supernatural occurred in evangelistic encounters. Acts 2 is classic. And later on in the book of Acts we see Peter raising the dead woman. As a result of that, two whole communities came to Christ.

In other words, when healing takes place it leads unto something. Jesus not only came to heal physically, but also the heart. We see it over and over again in the ministry life of Jesus and also the disciples following.

OBEYING THE WORD

When I began hearing the Lord regarding praying for the sick, I had no actual proof in my life or ministry that God would back up my actions when I began teaching on the works of the Kingdom. I've often been asked, "Did you experience a miraculous healing that led you into this ministry?" "Have you had a visitation from an angel?" "Did a divine healer lay hands on you and impart his anointing to you?" These kinds of questions presupposed a theology that to participate in Jesus' ministry I needed some kind of spiritual experience to initiate my ministry.

My response to these kinds of questions was a simple, "No. It's in the Book, so I do it." I was obeying Scripture because I believed that if Jesus said it and did it, then I should do it. This is important because it answers a common criticism that some have leveled at others and me.

Some contend that we start with our experience and then turn to Scripture to support it. The exact opposite was true for me. Instead, I started with the Bible, especially the gospels. I chose to obey the commands of Jesus without knowing whether or not we would see any results. And it was only when I tried to emulate Jesus' words and works in my life that my experience changed. I did not have a climactic moment of holy electricity that caused me to find texts to support my experience.

Every week I would teach from Scripture and then I would give an opportunity for people to come forward who needed prayer for healing. At one point, I became completely discouraged. We had been praying for the sick for nine months and had yet to see anyone healed of anything, not even a headache! Some of our friends left the church out of frustration and irritation. I wanted to quit. How could I keep teaching on healing when no results were backing it up?

It was then I sensed the Lord asking me, "Do you want to

teach my Word or your experience?" I knew the answer. There was no turning back. Whether or not Jesus ever answered our prayers with healing, it was my job to obey His mandate. After that dry spell the Lord finally healed a woman with the flu. I remember hooting to the Lord, "We got one! All right!" And the flow hasn't stopped ever since.

Most people that attend my healing seminars don't necessary attend for their own personal healing, but rather to learn how to pray for the sick. At these seminars when I do call forward the sick for prayer, it is to demonstrate healing and by example to teach others about divine healing. I rarely personally pray while I describe to the seminar participants what they are doing and why they are doing it.

I do not hold healing services so much as equipping seminars, where everyone learns how to exercise the power God makes available to us. Our trust is demonstrated by action.

Our trust is demonstrated by action.

In her book, *Chasing the Dragon*, Jackie Pullinger-To writes about her ministry to Chinese prostitutes. As a young girl she answered God's call to take the Gospel to the most decadent in Hong Kong's ghettos. Jackie has told me that many times Christians ask her, "How can you do it?" And Jackie responds by saying, "How could you not do it? How can we not pray for the sick?" I am not implying that everyone we pray for will be healed—surely they are not! But I am asserting that Scripture never qualifies who will be healed. Our task is to pray; God is the one who heals.

We cannot do or teach less than what is in the Bible. The reason all Christians can effectively pray for the sick and suffering is because we are empowered by the Holy Spirit, which is very important in healing ministry: "You will receive power when the Holy Spirit comes upon you" (Acts 1:8). Jesus told the disciples shortly before Pentecost.

And Paul writes that we are given gifts of healing from the Holy Spirit: "To one there is given through the Spirit the message of wisdom, to another the message of knowledge by means of the same Spirit, to another faith by the same Spirit, to another, gifts of healing by that one Spirit" (1 Corinthians 12:8-9). God's power, not human power, is the source of all divine healing. Our responsibility is to open our lives to the Spirit, to trust and honor him, and receive his power in our midst.

So often I meet pastors who believe in healing but never do it. Their services are timed to a gnat's eyebrow and there's no time left to pray for the sick. They move through the schedule and then they wonder why their church has no supernatural dynamic.

Do you know what gets me up every morning? I love this stuff! Hot dog—which, of course, is a theological term—I get to tell them about Jesus! This is good stuff. I want to encourage people on toward God, and all His blessings, including His power through healing. What an awesome and great deal for us to be in on!

GOD'S HEALING POWER

In October 1985 I was in England for three weeks, teaching at conferences in London, Brighton, and Sheffield. Many people were healed. One was not—me. During the previous two years I had suffered minor chest pains every four or five months. I suspected they had something to do with my heart but did nothing about them. Nobody, not even Carol, my wife, knew about my condition. But in England I could no longer hide it from her. On several occasions when we were walking I had to stop abruptly because of the chest pain. I was very tired most of the trip. I had what doctors later suspected were a series of coronary attacks.

When we returned home to Yorba Linda, California, Carol

insisted that I see a doctor. On November 3, I began a series of medical tests that culminated in a cardiologist's diagnosis that confirmed my worst fears: I had a damaged heart, possibly seriously damaged. Tests indicated that my heart was not functioning properly and possibly caused by high blood pressure. These problems, combined with my being overweight and overworked, meant I could die at any time.

My doctor told me that I needed to control my blood pressure by taking medication and reducing my salt intake, to begin walking daily, and to lose weight. Furthermore, he said that if I went on living at the pace at which I had been for years (in 1985 I was away from home for over forty weeks), I would most likely die from the results of stress. I complied with all of his directions.

> I believe I felt subconsciously that I deserved my condition and that to pray for healing was to pray against what I deserved. I had eliminated the possibility of God's forgiveness and grace for God's healing in my life.

But in my heart I felt different and I did not comply with God's direction to seek Him for healing. People prayed for me, but I lacked faith to receive divine healing. These words may sound strange, but I in fact found it difficult. Why? Because all of my life I have been a compulsive person, always working and eating more that I should, and I felt it was just that my body had finally started to break down.

I believe I felt subconsciously that I deserved my condition and that to pray for healing was to pray against what I deserved. I had eliminated the possibility of God's forgiveness and grace for God's healing in my life. This also meant that I found it easier to hear and follow doctors' orders than receive healing prayer because I felt the medical treatment and regimen were discipline for my wrongdoing.

There was nothing rational or reasonable about the way I felt and believed. For years I had known and taught Romans 8:1-2:

> *Therefore, there is now no condemnation for those who are in Christ Jesus, because through Christ Jesus the law of the Spirit of life set me free from the law of sin and death.*

But knowing in the head is not the same as believing in the heart. And the Lord had to reveal to me that it was His desire to heal me, not because of anything I was or wasn't doing; but just because that's what He likes to do; He loves healing people!

JESUS' PERSPECTIVE ON HEALING

Jesus was motivated to heal people not only because of His love for them, but also because of His hatred of the forces that bound them. A word of rebuke was often on the lips of Jesus when He was dealing with demons. The first demon Jesus met at the beginning of His ministry started to scream, until Jesus rebuked him (see Luke 4:35). Jesus did this on other occasions, once even rebuking a fever as if it were an animate thing that could respond to the orders of Jesus (which it did in Luke 4:39). Another time Jesus rebuked the elements of nature that were about to sink the boat He and the disciples were in (see Luke 8:24).

There is other evidence that Jesus was hostile to the forces of evil besides the specific use of the word "rebuke." One instance of this comes from Mark 3:1-6. Here we see Jesus in a synagogue on the Sabbath day. A man with a paralyzed hand was there, and the Pharisees were watching to see if Jesus would heal on the Sabbath. Jesus called the man to come up front and told him to stand there. He then turned to His antagonists and asked them if the law permitted one to do good on the Sabbath.

The Philips New Testament says: "There was a dead silence." Then Jesus, deeply hurt as He sensed their inhumanity, looked around in anger at the faces surrounding Him, and said to the man, "Stretch out your hand." Here we find one of the few times when Jesus is said to be angry at their lack of compassion.

Jesus healed because He was opposed to anything which bound or enslaved men.

Jesus healed because He was opposed to anything which bound or enslaved men. He recognized that the forces of darkness were in some way connected with the man's physical infirmities, and in opposing these infirmities, He was in essence showing His opposition to Satan and his kingdom.

Everywhere Jesus went He functioned as a healer. Forty-one distinct instances of physical and mental healing are recorded in the four gospels, but this by no means represents the total. Many of these references summarize the healing of large numbers of people. The accounts described in detail are simply the more dramatic instances of the healing ministry of Jesus. Toward the end of his account of the life and ministry of the Savior, John writes:

> *Many other signs Jesus also performed in the presence of His disciples, which are not written in this book. But these have been written that you may believe that Jesus is the Christ, the Son of God, and that believing you may have life in His name. ... Jesus did many other things as well. If every one of them were written down, I suppose that even the whole world would not have room for the books that would be written.*
>
> *– John 20:30-31; 21:25*

Nearly one-fifth of the gospel accounts are devoted to Jesus' healing ministry and the discussion occasioned by it. Out of 3,779 verses in the four gospels, 727 relate specifically to the healing of physical and mental illness or the resurrection of the dead. Except for a discussion of miracles in general, the attention devoted to the healing ministry of Jesus is far greater than that devoted to any other kind of experience.

Jesus came not only to bring the Kingdom of God, to save and to heal people, but also to impart to others this healing ministry that they might share in bringing people under the rule of God. We, as the Church, were commissioned by Jesus almost 2,000 years ago to announce the good news to all creation through the healing signs that would accompany and authenticate the message wherever it was preached. Today we find that about half the world's population has yet to hear the good news about Jesus. Therefore, the transference of Jesus' healing ministry to others (the Church) and the powerful exercise of it today are of utmost importance if we hope to see the Kingdom of God reach the ends of the earth.

Jesus transferred His healing ministry only after he had adequately modeled it. He chose and called twelve disciples with the purpose that they should first be with Him, and then be sent out to heal. They learned first by watching Jesus model healing. Everyday while living with Jesus they saw the power, joy, responsibility, strain, and tiredness involved in healing. They learned from His example exactly what to do. Jesus' method was clearly to minister while His disciples watched. He then would have them minister with Him watching them or receiving their reports. He would then leave them on their own to do it themselves.

As you go, preach this message: 'The kingdom of heaven is near.' Heal the sick, raise the dead, cleanse those who have leprosy, drive out demons. Freely you have received, freely give.

– Matthew 10:7-8

WE ARE TO PRAY FOR THE SICK

My perception is that often the ministry of the Spirit in any of the gifts such as healing, miracles, or the word of knowledge will precipitate an opening in people's lives that may result in their trusting in Christ as their life. Power evangelism means offering an explanation of the hope of the Gospel on the level of ordinary discourse, and an accompanying manifestation of the presence of God on the supernatural plane that quickens the people in their response. Healing should normally come not only through a few gifted individuals but through the entire church. Let's look at the variety of ways in which God's healing gift can manifest itself in the life of a receptive church.

First of all, I believe that there is such a thing as pastoral healing. That is to say, we have those that have been called by the Holy Spirit, gifted as it were, to minister to elders, pastors, and teachers.

Under the auspices of James 5 we have a responsibility to minister healing in an almost sacramental dimension—some would certainly call it sacramental. Additionally, I believe that there are those according to 1 Corinthians 12:28 that are called to the ministry of healing and miracles, and they may not necessarily be elders, pastors, or teachers. These people have been designated by the Spirit of God, gifted, and called to the ministry of healing in the same way that some people are called to the ministry of personal evangelism.

Another dimension of healing is that everyone in the body of Christ has the role and the potential gifting for healing. I believe that we've all been called to the responsibility of praying for the sick, for our immediate family and friends we work with. In any kind of situation—at work, at play, in recreation sites, or any place else—we are to pray for the sick as the occasion permits.

About two years before we began to see healings in our church, the Lord had burned indelibly in my mind Ephesians 4:11-12. God has given to the church: apostles, prophets, evangelists, pastors, teachers for the equipping of the saints to the ministry.

I had been working on models for equipping the saints at every level; teaching Bible studies, facilitating home groups, doing pastoral counseling, engaging in evangelistic work. The idea of adding healing to the list just seemed natural. You teach the people to do all the other things, why can't you teach them to heal the sick?

WATER WALKING

Learning how to heal is like learning how to walk on water. In both areas it is useful to know relevant biblical principles, to understand that Jesus is the Lord of all creation, and to talk to others who have been successfully involved in the activity. It can even be helpful to compare notes on why various approaches succeed or fail. When the time comes "to get out of the boat," however, all the best ideas and insights on "water walking" are of very little value.

The ability to successfully transcend the laws of nature is not discovered by mastering techniques or methodologies. When it comes to ministering in the power of the Holy Spirit, many people know why certain things can or should happen, but few people actually see them happen in their own experience.

The how of the healing ministry of Jesus is a mystery! But there is an even more perplexing question—why? Why would Jesus pass the wonderful privilege of continuing His healing ministry along to His followers? We're not sure; we only now that He has chosen to do so!

There are painfully few members of Christ's body who are responding in obedience to Him by choosing to move into the realm of the miraculous. Remember, eleven of the disciples stayed in the boat; only Peter ventured out onto the water. As a result it was Peter alone who enjoyed the privilege of overcoming the laws of nature in response to the Lord's call.

A ministry in the Spirit is withheld from those who seek to perform it in the power of the flesh. Pride and ambition are hindrances in the spiritual realm. A person who seeks to share the glory along with the risen Lord is limiting his usefulness to God. Sadly, many who are greatly used in healing ministry succumb to the subtle and destructive error of pride. Occasionally what begins in the Spirit unfortunately ends up in the flesh. Knowing the potential for casualties, we should approach a ministry of healing with reverence and sincere dependence on the Holy Spirit.

Jesus is still doing today what He was doing on the storm-tossed Sea of Galilee—calling common people to move above and beyond so-called natural laws and walk with Him in the realm of the miraculous. In the realm of the Spirit one thing is certain: Much more is unknown than is known! But our Lord is still calling us to follow Him.

THE ANOINTING OF THE HOLY SPIRIT

The ministry of healing was carried out through the followers' assertive trust, quickened by the guidance and anointing of the Holy Spirit. The main elements in carrying out the healing ministry by them to whom it was imparted were faith and the anointing of the Spirit e.g., when Peter and John healed the man at the gate called "Beautiful," Peter explains that it was not because of their spirituality, but Jesus' name and faith in His name that made the man whole.

It is the prayer of faith that saves the sick; therefore, assertive faith means a confidence without need of proof or regard for evidence, a conviction of truth and willingness to stand by it. There were obviously other elements present in this healing. They spoke a word, laid hands on the man, but all was done by the direction and anointing of the Spirit. This resulted in a quickening of faith, either in the recipient or the healer. Another point of importance is that when the disciples ministered, they did so in teams.

HEALING AND PRAYER LIFE

Prayer as it relates to healing is stressed throughout the New Testament. It was particularly marked in the life of Jesus. On one occasion Jesus inferred that prolonged prayer may be a necessary element in very difficult cases of healing (see Mark 9:29). It is interesting to trace prayer in the life of Christ, especially as it relates to His healing ministry.

Luke seems to make a point in this regard. Luke was captivated with the relationship between Jesus' ministry and the Holy Spirit. He seems to imply the same in regard to prayer. At Jesus' baptism Luke says that Jesus was praying. Before Jesus launched into His ministry, He spent forty days in the wilderness fasting and praying. The next mention of prayer by Luke is of Jesus getting up early in the morning for a quiet time alone with God prior to a very crowded and busy schedule of ministry (see Luke 4:42). Then he tells us about the crowds of people that came to hear Jesus and to be healed, and how He withdrew from them to pray (see Luke 5:15). Jesus prayed all night before selecting the twelve apostles whom he sent out to preach and to heal (see Luke 6:12-16).

The vital relationship between the prayer life of Jesus and His power-filled ministry, both in teaching and in healing, provides a helpful model for the Church today. Good preaching to some extent at least can be developed through close study and application of sound principles of speech, homiletics, and communications, but the awesome demands of ministering to someone who is hurting can only be met by an active and believing prayer life.

Learning to use the weapon of prayer in the healing ministry is certainly not unrelated to other aspects of the Christian life. The failure to be actively engaged in one aspect of the Christian life tends to affect the whole. Active, believing prayer included in the ministry of Christian healing will add a new vibrancy to all aspects of the life of the Church.

MINISTERING TO THE WHOLE PERSON

When we reach out and minister to others, an important principle when praying is to know that God is interested and wants to heal the whole person, not just specific conditions. In John 7:23 Jesus asked the Jews who had just accused Him of being demonized, "Why are you angry with me for healing the whole man on the Sabbath?"

The Greek word *hugies* translated "healing" reflects a much more comprehensive understanding of health than that of modern popular thought. Commenting on this and other Greek words used in the New Testament for health, John Wilkinson writes:

> *Health is thought of in terms of wholeness, well-being, life, strength and salvation. ... What modern man confines to the body, the Bible extends to the whole of man's being and relationships. It is only when man's being is whole and his relationships right that he can be truly described as healthy.*

I once heard someone say that it's more important to know what kind of person has the bug than what kind of bug has the person. By that he meant it is more important that we have information about a person's relationship with God and other people than that we have technical details about his or her illness. It is most important to keep in mind that we pray for persons and not simply conditions; this ensures the protection of people's dignity.

When we pray for a person's healing our goal should be that no matter the outcome—healed or not—that we are to leave him or her feeling more loved by God than before we prayed. One of the ways I express God's love is by showing interest in every aspect of the person's life. Often this means that praying for the sick takes a great deal of time, both in initial and follow-up prayer sessions. However, if it's the person God's interested in, we should then look upon him or her with the love and concern that Jesus has for them.

HEARING GOD FOR HEALING

The most fundamental skill required for healing is openness to the Holy Spirit, emptying oneself and receiving His leading and power. Frequently I encounter people who want a method for healing, a formula they can follow that guarantees them automatic healings. But divine healing is neither automatic nor dependent on our right actions; it is rooted in a relationship with God and the power of His Spirit.

Divine healing is a gift from God, an act of His mercy and grace. Our part is to listen to Him and carry out His Word. "He has made us competent as ministers of a new covenant," Paul writes, "not of the letter, but of the Spirit; for the letter kills, but the Spirit gives life" (2 Corinthians 3:6).

There are many ways in which we practice being open to God's presence and grow in hearing His words—Scripture study, worship, prayer, and mediation.

When I speak of listening to God's voice, I mean developing a practice of communion with the Father in which we are constantly asking, "Lord, what do You want me to do now? How do You want to use me? How should I pray? Whom do You want me to evangelize? Is there someone You want to heal?"

Sometimes the Holy Spirit gives me specific insights about people for whom I am praying. These come as impressions—specific words, pictures in my mind's eye, or physical sensations in my body that correspond to problems in their bodies. These impressions help me know who and what to pray for as well as how to pray.

I do not imply that I have an infallible "hotline" to God, and that I always hear His voice and follow His leading. But I am open to God, listening to Him, confident that He wants to lead us to minister to others.

> *The Counselor, the Holy Spirit, whom the Father will send in my name, will teach you all things and will remind you of everything I have said to you.*
> *— John 14:26*

> *But when he, the Spirit of truth comes, he will guide you into all truth. He will not speak on his own; he will speak only what he hears, and he will tell you what is yet to come. He will bring glory to me by taking from what is mine and making it known to you. All that belongs to the Father is mine. That is why I said the Father Spirit will take what is mine and make it known to you.*
> *— John 16:13-15*

LOOKING FOR FAITH

Whenever I'm praying for the sick I keep my eyes open to look for a healing environment, and an atmosphere full of faith and hope. I consciously look for faith in three places:

First, I look for faith in myself and others who are praying for the sick.

Second, I look for faith in the person being prayed for.

Third, I look for faith happening in those who are witnessing it taking place.

Usually I ask the person for whom I am praying, "Do you believe that Jesus can heal?" If he or she answers positively, I then ask, "Do you believe Jesus will do it now?" If the answer is yes or if a witness or I have a strong sense that God wants to heal, I go forward with healing prayer. I always look for faith and gather people with faith for healing. If no one has that sense, I ask God for the faith. I never blame the sick person for lack of faith if healing does not occur.

"Now faith," writes the author of Hebrews, "is being sure [of the substance] of what we hope for and certain of what we do not see" (Hebrews 11:1). I am rarely successful when that substance, that confidence of faith, is absent. I have been in many healing situations where, like Jesus, I have asked those who are struggling with unbelief, fear, or anxiety to leave.

At the same time I ask others who I know have faith for healing to join us. I have also observed that frequently one healing is a springboard to many others. When a group sees someone healed, their faith increases greatly, resulting in a healing environment.

During the time of prayer for healing I encourage people to "dial down," that is, to relax and resist becoming worked up emotionally. Stirred up emotions rarely aid in the healing process and usually impede learning about how to pray for the sick. So I try and create an atmosphere that is clinical and rational while at the same time powerful and spiritually sensitive. Of course, emotional expression is a natural by-product of divine healing and not a bad response. Artificially creating an emotionally charged atmosphere militates against divine healing and undermines training others to pray for the sick.

Finally, one of the most significant ways to increase faith for healing is worship. As we draw close to God, His Spirit works in us. Worship draws us into intimacy with the Father. It reminds us that He is God and we are not. But worship that draws us close to His heart can often give us clarity into what the Father is wanting to do.

This is especially important when we are praying for the chronically ill. Most Christians have friends or family members who have suffered from an infirmity, multiple infirmities, or a series of infirmities for many years. In some instances they have been prayed for divine healing literally hundreds of times without seeing any results. Frequently they give up hope for healing, resigning themselves to accept their condition or refusing further healing prayer. Who can blame them?

This is not to imply that Jesus never healed the chronically ill. For example, John 9 talks about Jesus healing a man blind from birth and also in Mark 5 where it speaks of the healing of a woman who had been bleeding for 12 years. In fact, of the 41 recorded instances of Jesus healing people, 33 appear to have been chronic cases. So, for those who have suffered for many years the possibility that God could bring them healing in this age is not excluded.

There is good news for those who are chronically ill. They should never give up receiving prayer for divine healing. But if in this age healing does not come, they are assured of their full restoration in the age to come. One common denominator in many of Christ's healings of the chronically ill was evangelism:

In 17 instances, healings took place in evangelistic settings (see Matthew 4:24; 8:16; 9:2-8; 9:32-33; Mark 1:23-28; 9:14-27; 10:46-52; Luke 8:42-48; 13:10-13, 16; 14:1-4; 17:11-19; John 4:28-30; 5:1-9,14; 9:1-7; Acts 3:1-10; 8:5-8; 14:8-10).

In 16 instances, the healings had an evangelistic result (see Matthew 9:2-8; 9:32-33; 12:9-13; Mark 1:23-28; 5:1-13, 18-20; 7:32-37; 9:14-27; Luke 5:12-14; 13:10-13, 16; 17:11-19; John 4:28-30; 9:1-7; Acts 3:1-8; 8:5-8; 9:32-35; 14:8-10).

In 21 out of 26 healings, there was either an evangelistic setting or result.

God seems to delight in healing difficult cases in evangelistic settings. These healings vindicate the preaching of the Gospel and the demonstration of God's power.

EVERYTHING POINTS TO THE CROSS

What about those who persevere in healing prayer and believe God for healing, yet still are not healed? The answer to this question is discovered in the relationship between divine healing and Christ's death on the cross. Theologians refer to Christ's death, the events surrounding it, and its results as the atonement. The Anglo-Saxon term "atonement" means "a making at one," indicating a process of bringing those who are estranged from God into unity with Him.

Sin is universal and cuts all men and women off from God. "When they sin against you—for there is no one who does not sin" (1 Kings 8:46a); "For all have sinned and fallen short of the glory of God" (Romans 3:23).

Sin is serious. "Your eyes are too pure to look on evil; you cannot tolerate wrong. Why then do you tolerate the treacherous? Why are you silent while the wicked swallow up those more righteous than themselves?" (Habakkuk 1:13). "Once you were alienated from God and enemies in your minds because of your evil behavior" (Colossians 1:21).

And sin is not something any of us can deal with by ourselves. "But if you fail to do this; you will be sinning against the Lord; and you may be sure that your sin will find you out" (Numbers 32:23). "Therefore, no one is declared righteous in his sight by observing the law, rather through the law we become conscious of sin" (Romans 3:20).

Jesus' atonement is central to our faith because though this action our sins are forgiven and we are brought back into right relationship with God.

Christ's death on the cross is the foundation of the Church, securing forgiveness and healing for our souls in this age. Everything in the Old Testament—especially the sacrificial system—points to the cross, and everything since then looks back to it.

Through the mystery of Christ's death, God revealed His love for us, as Paul shares, by delivering his Son "over to death for our sins" (Romans 4:25). Not only did Christ die for our sins, but also He died for us: "For Christ's love compels us, because we are convinced that one died for all, and therefore all died" (2 Corinthians 5:14).

So deep was His identification with us that He took our place in judgment. Paul goes on to say, "God made him who had no sin to be sin for us, so that in Him we might become the righteousness of God" (2 Corinthians 5:21). In fact, Peter teaches that this identification even touches the effects of sin in our physical bodies:

> *He Himself bore our sins in His body on the tree, so that we might die to sins and love for righteousness; by His wounds you have been healed.*
>
> *– 1 Peter 2:24*

Again, it's important to remember in praying for the sick, that whatever the condition, whatever ails them, it is always God's desire to heal them completely. So we continue to ask for healing, and we continue to press in by praying and ministering to those Jesus sends our way. If you ask Him, Jesus will give you opportunities by sending people your way that He wants to touch and heal.

Ten

Word and Works

"EVERYONE GETS TO PLAY"

Being on staff under John Wimber certainly could have its unplanned moments, and this particular day was no exception. It was your typical bright, blue-skied, southern California morning, and John and I were going ... somewhere. Every time I would ask where we were going, this mischievous smile would cross John's face—a smile that seemed to say, "I wonder how John Paul is going to handle this?"

On the freeway headed to Pasadena, he finally had mercy on me and matter-of-factly said we were going to Peter Wagner's Doctorate of Missiology class at Fuller Theological Seminary. I remember thinking, Wow! I've always wanted to see John in a classroom situation—*like the MC510 course he and Peter did in the early 1980s. But John quickly burst that bubble by informing me that he and I were going to speak on prophetic ministry—and I was going to demonstrate it. In a nanosecond I was cloaked in pure, unfeigned, mind-gripping terror!*

After we arrived and the class began, John gave a short overview—much too short, it seemed to me—of what prophetic ministry was to be in the Church and proceeded to ask me to speak on the gift of prophecy and how it works. I gave a much shorter version that I would today, as I was afraid everyone could see my knees shaking though my trousers. When I was done speaking, I turned to sit down, hoping John had changed his mind about the ministry time. But he hadn't. Discreetly, he took my arm, and whispered, "You'll be fine. The Holy Spirit is with you." And so, taking a deep breath, I slowly turned around and faced fifty or so students who were waiting for me to prove that God still spoke today.

It was then I felt John's thick hand on my back, and I could hear him praying in a whisper. John prayed like this the entire time

*I was ministering, his hand burning a hole in my back. By the end
of the ministry, under the power of the Holy Spirit, half the class
was weeping. Many were on the floor; others were sitting in
stunned silence. When the Holy Spirit lifted and I turned to go
back to my chair, John put his arm around my shoulders and qui-
etly said, "Never be afraid to minister like that. God is really with
you." I've never forgotten what John said to me that day, nor the
sound of his prayer, and sometime—when I'm more nervous than I
should be—I can still feel the touch of his hand.*

John Paul Jackson is a former Vineyard pastor and founder of
Streams Ministries International.

———◆———

Jesus, in the declaration concerning His mission, showed us
that there was both a spiritual and a social implication to
His incarnation. In His inauguration speech in Luke 4,
which is a restatement of Isaiah 61, He says that He has been
filled with the Spirit for a purpose: to bring the Good News to the
poor. And when Jesus ascended and commissioned us, He commissioned us to His ministry. Every now and then in a meeting
like this I will get someone who comes up to me and says, "Pray
for me that I'll discover my ministry." I'll say, "I don't have to
pray for that. There is only one ministry available, and it is the
ministry of Jesus. There has never been any other. But you can
participate in His. And if you will enter into His ministry, that's
where the joy is."

Jesus has come to set at liberty the oppressed and to proclaim
the acceptable year of the Lord. Now this term, "the acceptable
year of the Lord," refers to the year of Jubilee in which debts are
remitted, slaves are freed, and the land is redistributed.

Jesus Christ proclaims in this paragraph that it is established
now for all time. Part of what that means for us today is that we

can participate in not just a "hand out" but also a "hand up." We can train people and help them enter into life. I'm not saying that every poor person you meet is going to become a middle-class citizen—but I am saying that they probably can have a more productive existence after they meet you, if you go with the Gospel.

Jesus fulfilled his ministry by both word and deed, things He said and things He did. Matthew 4:23-25 says, "Jesus went throughout Galilee, teaching in their synagogues, preaching the good news of the kingdom, and healing every disease and sickness among the people." Word and works. One without the other is incomplete. It's both. To say, "God loves you" and not do any deeds of love is incomplete. It was an evidential kingdom: Jesus proclaimed the word of the Lord and did the deeds of the Lord, and everybody said, "Whoa! This is hot! This is a teaching, and with power!" They saw the demons come out. They saw the blind eyes see. They saw the lame walk, and they heard the Gospel of redemption and the call of God through Jesus Christ himself, to come and repent and to enter into the Kingdom, a kingdom that is "already" and "not-yet."

Jesus is fulfilling Old Testament prophecy about the Messiah that was to come. Psalms 84:14 tells us that it is a kingdom where righteousness and justice is the foundation of the throne, ruled by a king who says, "Let justice roll down like water and righteousness like an ever flowing stream" (Amos 5:24) and who upholds the cause of the oppressed and gives food to the hungry. To misuse or oppress the poor is to set yourself up for judgment. God will take up the cause of the poor; God Himself will vindicate. God Himself will bring things to the proper end.

We see in Isaiah 61 that Jesus declared he was sent to "preach the good news to the poor"—but not just the economically poor, or spiritually poor, but the poor in every way. The good news is for those who have been prepared by the Spirit and who are humble and receptive to the message of hope (see James 2:5).

The Church has been called to continue the ministry of Jesus by taking the same message of grace and blessing—the good news—to a dying world. "Good news" means eternal life, but that eternal life begins in this life; so the good news must be translated into a "language" people can understand.

For people in impoverished conditions, the good news may translate into food, clothes, help with shelter, and jobs. For people in the middle class, the good news will translate into something else. The Gospel is entirely sufficient for conversion, but wherever the Gospel is preached, God desires to redeem the whole man, not just the soul. History demonstrates that in a given context, as more individuals submit to the Kingdom of God, over time the circumstances of individuals, families, tribes, and even nations are enhanced.

Preaching the Gospel is all encompassing. It's telling people about Jesus, and salvation, but it's also feeding the hungry and praying for the sick. All these come under the banner of the "Good News." Furthermore, Jesus was sent to proclaim release to the captive. He came to earth with the power and authority to release people kept in bondage through "every disease" and "every sickness" (see Matthew 4:23). Matthew purposely used terms of a general nature, indicating the broad scope of Jesus' ministry, not the narrowness. Thus, Jesus brings a measure of release to the gamut of maladies in which people find themselves entangled, whether they are a direct result of human or demonic oppression. There are many different kinds of prisoners ... not all are behind bars.

> **There are many different kinds of prisoners ... not all are behind bars.**

Jesus was also sent to bring "recovery of sight to the blind." Blindness was only one of the many kinds of diseases that Jesus healed. Citing His Messianic credentials to the disciples of John the Baptist, Jesus said, "The blind receive sight, the lame walk, those who have leprosy are cured, the deaf hear, the dead are raised and the good news is preached to the poor" (Matthew 11:5).

More pervasive than physical blindness is spiritual blindness, which is blindness of the soul (see 2 Corinthians 4:4). Jesus addressed both kinds of blindness, and His church continues to do the same.

The Son of God was also sent to "release the oppressed." Christ came to liberate mankind from the penalty of sin, and release individuals from the consequences of sin and the oppression of evil spirits. Oppression in the world manifests in many forms of economic, ethnic, political, religious, cultural, and demonic situations. Jesus came to set the prisoners free and proclaim the favorable year of the Lord. He has come to redeem and save them, forgive their sins, take them out of their plight, and set them on a new road leading ultimately to their total redemption and deliverance when Christ's Kingdom comes in its fullest.

One of the more powerful points Charles Van Engen makes in his thought provoking book, *God's Missionary People*, is that the role of the local church in the world involves the Church in an apostolate received from, guided by, and patterned after the mission of Jesus. The mission of the church is the continuance of the ministry of Jesus. We only have ministry insofar as we've entered into the ministry of Jesus. Jesus made it very clear that He expected His followers to continue the ministry He began after His ascension into heaven. "As the Father has sent me, I am sending you" (John 20:21).

WHAT IT'S ALL ABOUT

There are some basic things you ought to know about the Christian life, and as a believer there are some things you ought to do: You ought to be nice to your neighbors and treat your spouse and children well. You ought to keep your bodies reasonably clean, and your minds, and maybe your garage, as well. You ought to try to make a productive living. You ought to grow in the grace of God. You ought to learn how to pray. But at the end of the day, it's really not about those things. Those things are the passageways; they're not the room. This present order of things is not "it." What's coming is "it."

Some folks are going to stand before God empty-handed because they never served Him. After they did a little ushering or had been on a committee or two, they thought they had fulfilled their obligation to the church, and as an institution they probably had. But they didn't fulfill their obligation to the founder of the Church. They have been called to serve Him all their lives long, with all their heart and mind and soul and strength. Jesus came to this world and issued a mandate for justice. And though there continues to be injustice in the world now, there will be a day when the trumpet will sound, with a great shout from heaven, and Jesus Christ, King of kings, will set everything right—every economic injustice, every ethnic dispute, every wrong that has ever been done, because Jesus is the standard.

Every painful thing, every abusive act, every sinful deed, everything done in the dark will be brought into the light. On that day, we will rejoice to be part of what he has done in bringing the kingdom will of His Father to earth. And in this period between the cross and the Second Coming, we are to "occupy" until He comes. We are to be productively involved in bringing justice to all.

In Matthew 9:35-36, Jesus sees the people as "harassed and helpless," but those words as translated in the NIV are pretty weak. The Greek uses violent words: The people are held down! Pinned to the ground! Jesus is talking about people abused by humankind. He looked out over the city of Jerusalem, and He wept with compassion. He said they were like sheep without a shepherd; they had no one to protect them, feed them, care for them, or look after them.

Now, so many of us have come through a Christian ministry that has told us, "God loves you and has a wonderful plan for your life." It's been an entry point through which you move toward an improved quality of life. "You can have a better marriage, your children will obey you, you can drive a nicer car, upward mobility is part of the package." Not all of that is completely wrong—but it doesn't do justice to the Bible.

CHRIST-CENTERED WORKS

I challenge people who take the Scriptures as their guide to become "Word-workers." These are Christians who believe and do what it says in the Bible. They don't discount entire sections of the New Testament by declaring that the Holy Spirit isn't doing those things anymore.

Between classes at Fuller Seminary I often relaxed out on the lunch patio under the shady maples. On this particular day, I was speed-reading the Gospel of John in a new translation. Perhaps because I was reading quickly or because of the new language, John 14:12 caused me to suddenly drop dead in my tracks: "If you have faith in Me, you will do the same things that I am doing" (CEV). I had been taught the traditional cessationist view of supernatural works and had accepted the fact that this verse did not mean what it says—that we should be able to minister like Jesus. Signs and wonders had stopped at the end of the apostolic age, so I thought.

Yet at that instant, the text exploded before my eyes. Jesus did all kinds of things that I had never even attempted, like healing the sick, casting out demons, and cleansing lepers. I had taught and preached the Gospel but had never healed any kind of sick-

ness or disease. Tears streamed down my face. It was as if someone had punched me in the stomach. My walk is incomplete. I
cried to the Lord. The realization that I was not obeying the
Scripture and doing all that Jesus did hit me hard that day.

What I didn't discover until that day was that being a Christian
with an obedient walk also included the risks of believing and
doing those things that Jesus believed and did. That day I wrote
in the margin of my Bible, "I must learn to believe everything that
Jesus believed and learn to do everything Jesus did."

OTHERS-CENTERED

Do you know what doing the works of the Father looks like?
Ministry is—serving and caring for others. In our fellowship I will
often tell someone to "minister" to someone in need. "What will
I say?" he or she will often ask. "I don't have any good advice to
give them." Usually I will say something like, "Don't say anything, just take care of them". Hug them. Cry with them. Laugh
with them. Get them dinner. Mow their lawn. Fix their car.
That's ministry!

> Hug them. Cry with them. Laugh with them. Get them dinner. Mow their lawn. Fix their car. That's ministry!

Ministry means doing whatever is necessary to help others
overcome their problems and
grow in confidence and holiness. We grow like plants.
When you minister to some-
one you tend them like a garden. The ministry of a servant has a
lot more in common with the nurse-patient or parent-child relationship than it does with the social worker-client or psychother-
apist-neurotic relationship that are so often the models for "ministry" in the church.

The truth is that ministry is much more than wise council and inspired prayer. It includes these things, but most of the more important and necessary kinds of ministry is the simple practical stuff. Listening, babysitting, driving people around town. Ministry means taking care of people, putting them first. Ministry is the work of a servant. It's simple work but also hard work because it means putting yourself in the back seat, and that is never easy.

Jesus gave the ministry to committed people. The Twelve were called to commitment to the person of Jesus. They were basically a motley bunch with backgrounds varying from rough, to status quo, to radical. But through mutual commitment Jesus made disciples out of them. He developed character and leadership within them, yet when He sent them out they were by no means perfect. That is the risk of being involved with training.

The Seventy seemed to include a wider group of committed people in training who were sent out after the Twelve had done what Jesus did. After this it becomes clear that Jesus has given this healing ministry to the Church, and that any Spirit-filled believer can heal and minister to others. Jesus also transferred this ministry by commission and gifting. After He had modeled healing, He commissioned His disciples to go and heal and He gave them the power to do so. Therefore, they were operating with His authority (commission) and His power (gifting).

Since Jesus has left the earth, the impartation of His ministry has not changed. His commission still stands for all believers, and the gift of the Holy Spirit has been sent to empower us to fulfill the commission.

> *Then Jesus came to them and said, "All authority in heaven and on earth has been given to me. Therefore, go and make disciples of all nations, baptizing them in the name of the Father and of the Son, and of the Holy Spirit, and teaching them to obey everything I have commanded you. And*

surely I am with you always, to the very end of the age.
— Matthew 28:18-20

And these signs will accompany those who believe: In my name they will drive out demons, they will speak in new tongues, they will pick up snakes with their hands; and when they drink deadly poison, it will not hurt them at all; they will place their hands on sick people, and they will get well.
— Mark 16:17

YOU ONLY GET TO KEEP WHAT YOU GIVE AWAY

From the very onset we were operating with the supposition that this was for everybody. Ephesians 4:11-12 says, "God has given to the church: apostles, prophets, evangelists, pastors, and teachers "for the equipping of the saints to the ministry." Either by teaching Bible studies, running home groups, doing pastoral counseling, or doing evangelistic work everyone is supposed to learn to do this, but I learned a basic Kingdom premise is you only get to keep that which you give away. I already knew that through evangelism you gave away your faith and your faith was sharpened in the process. I knew that by teaching you give away the things that nurture you, in the process yours are replenished. I found out the same thing was true in the leadership dimension: I had to give it away in order to see it multiplied and spread.

I think it is very, very helpful when a pastor decides to initiate or introduce this kind of healing ministry, to give it plenty of time, a period of months, even years, to teach and communicate on a sharing level with the most receptive leaders in the church. Give them the same information that you're getting; the same thing that has produced a new posture or position in you will produce the same thing in them (your people). Share the information; share the experience.

Pastors have come to us over the years for help with learning to pray for the sick, and we just tell them, "Well, just come and visit. Watch us do it, and once you've watched us do it, get some of your people, your leaders, to come in and also watch us do it." Then, as I would tell them, "When your leaders have watched us do it, you begin trying it on a small scale. Don't launch a big campaign in which you try to get the whole church committed at once. Go home and begin by putting a slot in once a week where you'll pray for the sick. As God begins healing, give visibility to that. Let people testify to what's happened in their lives and introduce it slowly over a period of time." I wouldn't recommend that others do it the way I did it. I said to our church, "This is the way to do it." I think we unduly pressed people to get involved in it or get out the door.

How do we do it? Having small groups was part of our history. We have been in small groups most of our Christian life. So, I said, "The best place for trial and error is the small group. That's where we'll start doing this as much as we are able to."

INSTRUCTION AND DIFFICULTIES IN MINISTRY

Jesus not only commissioned the disciples and believers for ministry, but He also left instructions. He told them where and to whom they should go, which He still does today, every day through His Spirit in the hearts of listening believers. They were to pronounce the Kingdom of God upon the recipients and give healing freely, no matter what the need was, because they also had received freely. A simple lifestyle of trusting God, traveling light and healing the sick was developed. They were to give themselves to the hospitality and the support of receptive people, and to avoid wasting time with persons who might rejects God's Kingdom. Persecution was to be expected; therefore, they were to operate wisely and keep their innocence. The Holy Spirit within us is our helper and instructor for every situation.

Those to whom this ministry was given encountered difficulties. Their initial excursion was greeted with great success and joy. Even the demons were subject to them in Jesus' name! However, they soon encountered difficulties with their own pride and carnality, e.g., trying to stop others who were healing in Jesus' name. They lapsed back into unbelief and Jesus had to rebuke them (see Mark 9:38-40).

The early church also encountered vicious persecution, especially from the religious leaders of the day. So don't be surprised that when you step out in ministry, you will encounter some opposition. Much of the time I realize that when I'm moving and stepping out in obedience to minister, I can expect that there will most often be some opposition of some kind.

> *Remember the words I have spoke to you: "No servant is greater than his master." If they persecuted me, they will persecute you also. If they obeyed my teaching, they will obey yours also. They will treat you this way because of my Name, for they do not know the One who sent me.*
>
> *– John 15:20-21*

GLORIOUS ANTICIPATION

I have spent a lot of time and energy learning about Jesus' second coming, the rapture, and the tribulation. I was weaned as a baby Christian on all the best-known teachers of the second coming of Jesus. It was and still is a subject that truly excites me!

However, after several years of hearing many debates on whether there would be a rapture before, during, or after the tribulation, I simply grew tired waiting for Jesus. I decided it was time I seriously looked into the bulk of Scripture dealing with the Christian's lifestyle and ministry.

I discovered that Jesus said this regarding the end times: "And this gospel of the kingdom will be preached to the whole world as a testimony to all nations, and then the end will come" (Matthew 24:14). Jesus clearly links the end times to the completion of a task. That task is the extending of God's rule upon the earth in the words and works of the Kingdom!

This message and the ministry of the Gospel are to be taken to the whole world by each generation of the church until He comes! Jesus wants us to be committed to His second coming and be prepared at all times. And He also wants us to be committed to speaking His words and doing His works until He returns!

In Acts 13, the Holy Spirit set aside Paul and Barnabas from the church at Antioch and called them out to become traveling ministers of the Gospel. Today the Holy Spirit continues this unique ministry of calling believers to go.

At the Anaheim Vineyard in 1984, we were finally getting settled in a building that could accommodate our rapidly growing fellowship. At the same time the Holy Spirit began to accelerate this ministry of calling out many of our people to leave the fellowship and to go to other areas to start new fellowships. From as close as Yorba Linda, California (not far from our church in Anaheim) to Long Island, New York, many of our dearest friends followed God's call to pioneer new works.

At this time the Lord had spoken to us that this was just the beginning and that many more would be trained and sent out to start new fellowships. The Lord knew then what He had in mind for us in the Vineyard, but it took risk on our part to venture outside of what we even knew possible at the time (see Acts 13:3). It's always a risk to let people go, especially if they are your friends, but that is exactly what we are called to do. We give away our best, and in turn God always gives us more. It's just the part of keeping busy, doing the Kingdom work until the King comes back to get us.

The crux of Paul's advice to Timothy is found in 2 Timothy 4:2-5. Here Paul urges Timothy to be ready to preach the Gospel and minister "in season and out of season." The Gospel ministry, unlike fresh strawberries, is never out of season. We must be ready and willing the share the life and works of Jesus at anytime—when we "feel anointed" and when we don't "feel anointed," when we have the energy and when we don't.

The willingness to minister anytime takes self-discipline—a very unpopular lifestyle for many of us. We don't mind ministry when we feel like it, but ministry anytime? That would cramp our style! Yet, Hebrews 12:6-7 reminds us that "children of God who are not disciplined, live as if they have no father." We need to be under the rulership of our Father. When opportunities to minister come our way, it pleases the Father and we must obey. Ministry has no season!

Like young Timothy, we all need to be encouraged to persevere in the ministry to which God has called every believer. We can become discouraged and fearful when we face the inevitable hardships, resistant hostile people, and frustrations that often come in reaching out to people. These are just simply realities of ministering to others. Yet God, the Holy Spirit, the same Spirit who calls us to serve God, can renew our strength and remind us of the true and eternal value of our work.

Unless we proclaim Jesus in His fullness and continue His ministry, we haven't done the essential thing to affect the world around us.

This is an exciting time to serve God. Satan has overplayed his hand by brutalizing the people of the earth for centuries. The earth and its people are crying out for relief and salvation from the evil forces and destruction which continue to victimize them. God wants us to continue Jesus' ministry of liberation! To the sick and diseased, Jesus brought healing; to the spiritually oppressed, Jesus brought deliverance; to those separated from God, He brought forgiveness and restoration.

It was always Jesus' plan to continue to vanquish the power of the evil one by using flesh and blood people like you and me. There is no greater calling!

> *Do not neglect your gift, which was given to you through a prophetic message when the body of elders laid their hands on you. Be diligent in these matters; give yourself wholly to them, so that everyone may see your progress. Persevere in them, because if you do you will save both yourself and your hearers.*
>
> *– 1 Timothy 4:14-16*

'Gracelets'

"NATURALLY SUPERNATURAL"

Perhaps the central focus in John Wimber's leadership was that of "doing what the Father was doing" (which, he understood from John 5, was Jesus' main concern). However, John could not be content with simply growing in that ability himself; he was also passionately committed to the Great Commission—apprenticing others to the same growing experience of exercising Jesus' words and works. Practically, this meant that anyone who spent any considerable time with John would inevitably be drawn into a process of "show and tell" (modeling, explanation and practical risk-taking) that he saw as being Jesus' primary method of disciple-making.

I was one of those who had the great privilege of spending considerable time with John during the 80s and 90s and experienced first hand his conscious mentoring. Whenever possible, even in the middle of conference ministry times, John would draw me aside and ask, "What do you see God doing here?" When these "in the moment" dialogues were not possible, he intentionally focused our conversation afterward on that same question.

John realized that our human tendency "in the moment" is to see and hear at the most surface level of what is taking place. The fruit of human energy dominates our focus—we tend to see what people do and what people say. At best, when we gain some sense of the underlying spiritual dynamics, we primarily are aware of what God isn't doing and center on what Satan is doing to undermine the potential of God's activity. Believing that our task is always one of partnering with the work of God's Spirit, John would always stretch me to become more conscious of God's intention and activity, especially at an embryonic level. "Who is speaking God's wisdom right now?" he would ask me. "What is the level of faith in the room? Where is there faith to call for a display of God's Kingdom?" These kinds of questions (along with John's answers) helped me grow immensely in my own ability to see and hear what God was doing. I'm glad he persevered!

Gary Best and his wife, Joy, have planted many Vineyard churches across Canada. Gary is also National Team Leader of Vineyard Churches Canada.

———◆———

GOD'S GIFTS

by Carol Wimber

One of our highest values in the Vineyard is that each one does *their* own part in Kingdom work. John used to say that it's a word and works Kingdom. We preach the Gospel, heal the sick, feed the hungry, and clothe the naked. We do this in a naturally supernatural way. The angels by direction from the Lord do their part, too. These are all acts of service, simply gifts at work in the body of Christ, and it's not our job to make a show of it. We don't draw attention to ourselves, and we get rid of all the hype, all the theatrics. We tune it down, not up, in order to hear and see what the Father is doing, where the Father is at work.

I remember numerous times how John would have everyone take a coffee break just as the emotional atmosphere was sky high. And then, cold turkey, with no music, no anything, he would ask the Holy Spirit to come to heal and deliver. Emotion has nothing to do with power; it only has to do with humanity. This is neither right nor wrong, unless we think emotional intensity equates the power of God.

Everyone wanted to give John a title, but he was never up for it. He would say, "We don't use titles, just call me John." We don't print up cards saying, "Apostle Steve" or "Prophet Larry." We don't have designated elders because we didn't need to. John would say, "An elder is as an elder does. Let's see who elds." It was always functional. If someone was functioning in a certain way and it was working, John usually had this amazing sense to recognize it, bless it and oftentimes that is how our leadership team would come about. We have to be careful of the trap of authority positions. Jesus warned:

> *You know that those who are regarded as rulers of the Gentiles lord it over them, and high officials exercise authority over them. Not so with you. Instead, whoever wants to become great among you must be your servant, and whoever wants to be first must be a slave to all. For even the Son of Man did not come to be served, but to serve, and to give his life as a ransom for many.*
>
> *– Mark 10:42-45*

John never used the word "laity." The gifts of the Spirit are for every Christian—good Christians and bad Christians, new believers and old, mature disciples and immature babes in Christ. The gifts of the Spirit are for the receiver (the one being prayed for) so all that is required is that the messenger (the one praying) gets the package to the ones who God is sending it to. The gift says everything about the Giver and nothing about the messenger. The only thing required to be used of God to deliver a gift—be it healing, deliverance, prophecy, etc.—is to be available.

The Lord longs to bless His people, and He is moved by our suffering. Our loving Father looks for opportunities when we meet together and faith is present. The *charisms* (or "gifts") have been aptly described as the "dancing hand of God." Jesus loves to drop "gracelets" on the assembled people, and the Spirit loves to communicate this through willing hearers.

We don't carry the gifts around with us. They are not ours; they are God's gifts. Spiritual gifts are neither badges nor awards; they are simply tools that God gives us when needed. "The gifts are situational," John would often say. Being human, we hate that! It's uncomfortable because we don't get to carry them in our pocket; they are only here for the moment. It's a faith thing!

———◆———

As a young convert, I was often told that I was an evangelist because I led so many people to Christ. But I did not understand about gifts and ministry, and so I denied that I was an evangelist.

"Don't you lead people to Christ?" I was asked.

"Yes—but I thought we were all supposed to do that," I would respond.

I led people to Christ because I thought that witnessing was my duty. But my duty became my passion, and my passion became my ministry. For the first ten years after I became a Christian, evangelizing people was the focal point of my life. Because this is what I was actually doing over and over, it became my ministry. The Spirit bestows a gift and provides the occasions and opportunities for its use—then the repeated use of the gift creates a ministry.

Sheer effort of will often produces works that are naturally good. For example, many people are truly hospitable—generous, warm, kind, and considerate. Their hospitality is a blessing. I think of this as a role that all of us are called to. Everyone should anticipate serving in any and all ways, and we should anticipate any and all "gracelets" of the Holy Spirit as we go.

> *Now you are the body of Christ, and each one of you is a part of it. And in the church God has appointed first of all apostles, second prophets, third teachers, then workers of miracles, also those having gifts of healing, those able to help others, those with gifts of administration, and those speaking in different kinds of tongues. Are all apostles? Are all prophets? Are all teachers? Do all work miracles? Do all have gifts of healing? Do all speak in tongues? Do all interpret? But eagerly desire the greater gifts.*
>
> *– 1 Corinthians 12:27-31*

I see a distinction between spiritual gifts and ministries. When Paul asks if all are apostles, prophets, teachers and miracle workers, his answer is obviously no. This passage has often been misinterpreted and understood to be placing a limitation on the abundance of gifts. But I now see that these verses are Paul's word about church ministries. There should be people in each church appointed by God for these specific ministries.

For example, if an outstanding work of power takes place in one of the gatherings in our church, I can usually guess that one of five or six particular members happened to be praying for the person who received the miracle. These are the people in our church who have the ministry of miraculous powers. That is not to say that they walk around with miracles in their pockets. It is not a matter of aptitude. But while they're praying for people with coughs or backaches or other common ailments, they might come to someone with a far more significant problem—such as cancer or heart disease—and that disorder might be healed. We consider that a miracle.

Spiritual gifts are for use anywhere and anytime—in the streets, marketplace, at home, and, of course, in the Church. The apostle Paul's letter hardly gives the impression that in the Christian life some people are to be players and others are spectators. Christians are all players. Everyone is to participate. In a given church body, everyone can partake of the array of spiritual gifts. Then members are also called into particular ministries. Not everyone in a local church will be called to the ministry of evangelism, but a number of people will (Ephesians 4:11).

Not everyone in a local church will be called to the ministry of healing the sick, but a portion will, and they may function in teams and ministry groups (see 1 Corinthians 12:30). Not everyone in a church will be called to teach, but some will. Everyone has a place of service. We eagerly desire the spiritual gifts and are willing to move on into whatever ministries God wants for us.

Where churches are coming into this kind of maturity, they are having an increasing influence on the surrounding community. The gifts of the Spirit are not trophies, talents, traits, or toys. The gifts of the Spirit are God's supernatural expressions of love, caring, kindness, healing and concern, bestowed upon us and through us.

BEING PRACTICAL

The idea of a second work of grace—a subsequent experience to salvation needed to receive the Holy Spirit—is a major problem for many evangelicals. Evangelicals, through Scripture study, know that they receive the Holy Spirit when they are born again and therefore have great difficulty looking for a second work.

I maintain the evangelical position that the born-again experience is a consummate charismatic experience. Any ensuing interaction between the individual and God comes under the heading of "filling," as emphasized by Paul. If I take this posture then I must deal in some pragmatic way with what is meant by being born-again in the New Testament. If, as many evangelicals believe, the Acts 2 experience was the birth of the Church, it is therefore connected with the coming of the Spirit and spiritual gifts. My question to any evangelical is: "If that's true, then why aren't these gifts also in the Church today?"

I also believe it's important to emphasize the importance of expectation. If the experience of the Holy Spirit isn't preached or seen by the people, a trait sadly indicative of most evangelical churches, they won't expect these things to happen; therefore, they will not happen. When we see that there is more we can experience, we are willing to embrace the gifts and operate in them.

In the beginning of the 20th century there was a debate on whether the "Baptism of the Holy Spirit"—the commonly used term then—meant a heightened spirituality and sanctification, or if it meant power for ministry. I believe both sides are essentially correct. It does mean growth, sanctification, and spirituality. You will love the Lord more. You will pray more. You will be more vital and integrated into your community ... for having yielded more of your life to the Holy Spirit.

But it is also for a purpose beyond the embellishing of your Christian life, namely winning the lost and building churches. That's Jesus' point when He says, "You will receive power when the Holy Spirit comes upon you." It's not only something you do, but it's something you are. "You will be my witnesses in Jerusalem and Judea and in Samaria and to the ends of the earth" is the guy next to us at work, or that neighbor that maybe we haven't been so nice to, or that brother or sister that we've been estranged from for years.

So, the mighty work of empowerment and refreshing that we experience serves a purpose. In 1771 the British founder of the Methodist movement, John Wesley, commented

> **The mighty work of empowerment and refreshing that we experience serves a purpose.**

in a letter: "No part of Christian history is so profitable, is that which relates to great changes wrought in our souls: these therefore should be carefully noticed, and treasured up for the encouragement of our brethren." The Church is called to bear witness, make disciples and gather them into fellowships, starting new churches as necessary. Everything else we do—praying for the sick, feeding the hungry, and caring for one another—should advance us to that end.

It is very important to me that we have theological backing for what we practice. The evangelical Christian feels that he must have a theological basis for all practice, though many in fact do not believe this, but argue from experience instead. But nevertheless this is a commonly accepted idea. One thing that makes the Vineyard so unique in what we do is that in our church and in the class at Fuller Seminary where I taught, I operate with that basic approach: We move from the Scriptures to experience rather than vice versa.

When we first started teaching the "Signs, Wonders, and Church Growth" course, I had several delegations from classic Pentecostal denominations come and visit. During our class period when a delegation from a large Pentecostal denomination visited, a great deal of power came over the class. The presence of God was manifested in a very special way. Afterward, the Pentecostals asked me if we had ever had a "visitation." I answered "No". "You mean you haven't had an angel visit you?" Again I said, "No." "Were you healed of a major disease or disorder?" And I said, "No." Their question assumed that initiation is begun by some sort of experience—a divine interaction. I told them that the way I started was by reading from the Gospel of Luke. I was teaching from it and after the third chapter every few verses dealt with healing or some other supernatural occurrence. Once I saw that healing and moving in the gifts was a biblical norm, I had to deal with it in a practical way.

THE MANIFESTATION OF THE SPIRIT OF GOD

The manifestation of the Spirit is not supposed to be the exception; it is supposed to be the norm. How many of us has God given spiritual gifts? *To everyone!* Some might think, "Not to me. What Paul is talking about hasn't ever happened to me." My answer is, "Yes it has! You just didn't have the theology, the practice, or the encouragement to recognize it and respond."

Most of us, frankly, are just too dull and lethargic about our Christian witness and responsibility to be able to release the gifts.

Furthermore, many of us are ignorant about spiritual gifts simply because we have not received biblical teaching about them and have not seen healthy examples of them, "Now about spiritual gifts brothers, I do not want you to be ignorant" (1 Corinthians 12:1). It is part of the job of apostles, prophets, evangelists, pastors, and teachers to encourage and prod the Church to operate in the gifts, and now in many places today the Church is being encouraged and equipped to release the gifts.

Most of the models of spiritual gifts to which the evangelical community has been exposed are immature Christians—persons not formed in a godly character. What put me off for years as a pastor was the steady stream of people that would come to me after having been baptized with the Holy Spirit, who were now operating with an elitist attitude, telling me that I was not as spiritual as they were. Of course, I measured them on the basis of their family life and character—what I think are sound bases for judging growth and maturity of individuals—and I very often saw immature people.

But this was a false basis for judging the validity of spiritual gifts because gifts are not only given to mature people—they're given to willing people. It took several years for me to realize that these people had become barriers rather than bridges to my experiencing and understanding gifts. When I came to Fuller Seminary I became aware that some of my colleagues spoke in tongues. I recognized in them a mature character and lifestyle. I then dealt with the gifts.

> Spiritual gifts ... are not only given to mature people— they're given to willing people

The Spirit touches all of us in certain ways at various times, but most of us either have not known that or have not known what to do with it. Thus, many of us have experienced a moving of the Spirit and have suppressed it. For example, when we are suddenly able to apply Scripture to the private life of someone we are talking with, that ability is a spiritual gift. When we walk into a room and suddenly know secret facts about people in the room, that knowledge is a spiritual gift. This is how gifts work. They are manifestations of the Spirit that come on us and work through us. We may not have names for all the gifts, but we can see them functioning. All of us have had a few of these experiences, and we could have more of them if we were encouraged to have them. If we ask for the gifts and seek them, as the Scripture tells us to, we will get more of them.

One thing that may have prevented us from asking for the gifts is that we have been taught that they are related to personality traits. For example, if a person is always happy, he might be told that his spiritual gift is to be an encourager like Barnabas. Yet some of the best encouragers I know have not been particularly outgoing or positive people. But spiritual gifts as I am discussing them are independent of personality traits.

TALENTS: USE THEM OR LOSE THEM

If you think you are too ordinary and too humble to do anything for the Kingdom, go to Matthew 25 and reread the parable of the talents. This is the parable for the modest, apprehensive, ordinary Christian. It's for every man and woman who gets tongue-tied when eloquence is needed, who feels like running when that disturbed person comes in the door, who is convinced that he or she isn't bright enough, or doesn't know the Bible well enough, or feels like he doesn't have enough time to help out anybody.

In this story, the Master is going away for a while. He entrusts his property to three servants. One gets five talents; the second gets two; the third gets one. The master makes the division according to the servant's abilities. The more able servants do well. The most gifted servant wheels and deals, gets up early to read the *Wall Street Journal*, spends hours on the phone with the broker everyday, gets in the best tax shelters, and managed to double his master's money. His five talents become ten, and the master is delighted.

The second servant has less money to work with and is less sharp as an investor. He probably put the money in a safe but profitable portfolio of tax-free municipals, blue chip stocks, and money markets. But he doubled his money and the master was very pleased.

The third servant was afraid. As soon as the master left, the guy rushed off and buried his one talent in the ground. Years later, when the master asked for an explanation, the little guy explained that he didn't want to take any chances. "You are a hard man," he told the master, " and I didn't want to make any mistakes." "You bet I'm a hard man," said the master. "You could have at least put my money in savings and earned a little interest. Your fear got the better of you and that shows you are an unworthy servant." The whole point here is being faithful with what God entrusts to us.

And if you aren't doing anything for the Lord because you are afraid of messing up, making mistakes and looking like a fool, watch out! You will eventually have to give an account to God, and that's really something to be afraid of. Even if you only have on talent, the master expects you to use it. Use it or lose it. The choice is yours.

When I pray with evangelicals, I ask if they are born again and if they received the Holy Spirit when they received Christ. If they answer "yes," I tell them that all that remains is for them to actualize that which the Spirit has—all that is required is for them to release the gifts. I then lay hands on them and say, "Speak in tongues or prophecy," and they do. I always use those two gifts as initiatory because that seems to be the pattern in the New Testament.

I often see another theological barrier to spiritual gifts which are what I call an incorrect interpretation of 1 Corinthians 12:8-10 and 20-31 in which the gifts are frequently understood as given individually and unilaterally to each member of the body. My perception is that we have wrongfully interpreted that text. If we go back to 1 Corinthians 11:17-18, Paul says, "When you gather together there are divisions among you." The emphasis in the entire section (from chapters 11-14) is that he is speaking to the church corporately, the congregation at Corinth. Therefore, the emphasis on the gifts is that they are not primarily given to the individual but to the whole body.

IGNORANCE ABOUT SPIRITUAL GIFTS

First Corinthians 11:18 through 14:40 deals with abuse of the gifts and spiritual phenomena in the church at Corinth. Paul begins by addressing the issue of divisions among them. In Corinth, people were polarized along lines of personal allegiance (see 1 Corinthians 1:12), along economic lines (see 1 Corinthians 11:22), and apparently along lines of spiritual gifting.

In the chapter 12, Paul deals with ignorance concerning spiritual gifts in the first 11 verses. Paul uses the "body metaphor" to explain the exquisite interaction of the spiritual gifts. He talks about the eye, the ear, the nose, and the foot, and how we all need each other as a body. When we gather, there ought to be a functioning together for the edification and benefit of all. He hammers the theme of respecting, honoring, blessing, deferring, loving, edifying, and building up one another. Again, we use our spiritual gifts to edify and build up the whole church, not to lift up ourselves.

Using that criteria alone, the overall effect of this visitation has been overwhelmingly positive. There was some excessive enthusiasm going on at Corinth, and we see it from time to time in contemporary settings. But we can deal with it in a positive way that will encourage the ongoing dynamic of God's visitation among us. I've seen people strengthened and encouraged. I see a greater willingness for the saints to roll up their sleeves and work in various avenues of ministry. That reality, however, has to be weighed against the various and sundry instances of emotional excess.

On August 15, 1750, John Wesley wrote in his journal:

> *The grand reason why the miraculous gifts were so soon withdrawn, was not only that faith and holiness were well-nigh lost, but that dry, formal, orthodox men began even then to ridicule whatever gifts they had not themselves and to decry them all as either madness or imposture.*

Controversy has always surrounded spiritual gifts. When the Holy Spirit came on Pentecost and many spoke in tongues, there were witnesses who accused them of drunkenness. When the "apostles performed many miraculous signs and wonders," the people became fearful (see Acts 5:11-13). Nevertheless, many were healed and delivered of evil spirits—and "more and more men and women believed in the Lord and were added to their number" (Acts 5:14).

It didn't help that some Christians abused the gifts. In his first letter to the Corinthians, Paul addresses—among other issues—the misuse of the gifts. First Corinthians 12 and 14—the two most prominent passages found in the New Testament on the gifts—are sandwiched around Paul's memorable words of love in chapter 13. The context is clear: Without love, the gifts are of no value.

WESTERN WORLDVIEW

Western Christians often hold a worldview that inhibits their ability to interpret and submit to Scripture correctly. This is a deeper problem than the philosophical issue of secular humanism; it is the ever-increasing domination of Western materialism. By that I mean that we have come to a place where our worldview is more empirical than cosmic. Most Western Christians hold a cosmic perception of Scripture. We believe that Jesus really did interact with demons, spirits, and angels. Yet at the same time, many deny any possibility of that kind of experience today because they have been affected by a materialistic worldview in which anything experienced outside of our five senses is suspect. In this sense, much of the church today is secularized.

Missionaries leaving Western culture and entering a developing nation or Eastern society are introduced to a different worldview than we have, one that makes room for the supernatural. They are frequently overwhelmed by what they experience. They are not trained to deal with this, and very little that they've trained in has effect there. Consequently there is a turnover of 80-90 percent of all first-term missionaries.

Chuck Kraft tells about going to Nigeria and trying to teach from Romans to the Nigerians. After a few months, they came to him, very politely, and said that they appreciated his teaching but it was not relevant to their needs. What they needed was wisdom for dealing with spirits that plagued the villagers every night.

Our worldview controls our theology, but more importantly it controls our practice. Our missionaries come back from their jaunts and, except in private circles, never tell stories about the supernatural interaction that occurs in the field because they know that their constituency would resist them. Since they are financially dependent on the constituency, they cannot risk disrupting the money flow. So many say nothing. Supernatural gifts represent a disruption to the Western worldview. Speaking in tongues and prophesying create a major tension for our basic assumption about how things are supposed to operate in the Western world.

ORDER IN THE CHURCH

We don't have a New Testament text that prescribes what elements a New Testament worship service must have, but many Scriptures give us enough to form an outline. For example we find Scriptures that talk about worshiping God through song (see Colossians 3:16; Acts 16:25; Ephesians 5:19). These and many other Scriptures formed the building blocks of our theology of worship, helping us to understand worship as our first priority.

Other elements of the church gathered can be found in:
- Preaching: 1 Timothy 4:13, 5:17
- Teaching: Acts 2:42
- Fellowship: Acts 2:42
- Breaking of Bread: Acts 2:42
- Prayer: Acts 2:42; 16:25
- Reading of Scripture: 1 Timothy 4:13
- Collecting tithes, offerings & alms for the poor: Romans 15:25-27; 2 Corinthians 9:7; 1 Timothy 9:8

Then there's what we would call the gifts or ministry area of gathering (1 Corinthians 12:8-11):
- Revelation
- Knowledge
- Prophecy
- Prophecy with Interpretation
- Tongues/Interpretation
- Healing
- Deliverance

All these things are normative activities of the church. Do Paul's prescriptions in 1 Corinthians regarding the exercise of gifts in a public setting apply to any and every situation in which the body of Christ meets?

I don't think so. Different kinds of situations utilize different kinds of "order." The church can meet for a variety of purposes: prayer, funerals, and weddings. We meet for the purpose of evangelism. The church in Jerusalem met for distribution of food to the widows. The church carries out its mission in a variety of settings, each with its own proper sense of order. "Order" in one type of meeting will mean something different in another type. We have funerals in our church, and we have baptisms in swimming pools. Both gatherings are for important reasons, but what serves as order for one would be inappropriate for another.

Therefore, the expectations of what constitutes order in a meeting devoted to renewal may differ from a typical Sunday morning worship service that is open to the public. On certain occasions in Scripture, God demonstrates a different understanding of order than we have within our culture. Within the Western rational mind-set which most of us in the United States have inherited, we have some naturalistic assumptions. We usually think of everything in terms of cause and effect. Not everything we read about in Scripture fits within that framework. There are things where we can't see the cause and/or effect. Some things happen that cannot be explained.

For instance, 2 Chronicles 5 relates how the Ark of the Covenant was installed in the new temple. In the midst of resounding worship with musicians and singers, the text says that " ... the house of the Lord was filled with a cloud, so that the priests could not continue ministering because of the cloud; for the glory of the Lord filled the house of God" (vs. 13-14).

How would that fit into our culturally viewed understanding of "order"? We like things in a certain sequence, without surprises. We like things dished up in a certain way. I don't have any problem with that, but neither do I have a problem with having less order for short periods of time or a specific focus. Do you have tolerance for surprises and change? Even when we are surprised, having balance is important. In 1 Corinthians 14, Paul prescribes three earmarks of ministry in corporate gathering in the church: intelligibility, order, and edification.

When the Spirit is moving in a church made up of fallible human beings (that's all of them, in case you were wondering) there's potential for abuse. The answer is love, order, clarity, and edification. He gives a summary text in 1 Corinthians 14:40 that says, "But everything should be done in a fitting and orderly way."

We don't need to legislate what goes on in renewal meetings as long as the brethren are being built up and edified. However, we do need to administrate our meetings based on biblical discernment. Some people have more openness and ease in the presence of the "chaos" of the Spirit. Some have little tolerance for this activity. That's fine. But we must first learn, then minister to people at both ends of the spectrum—and everyone in between. Some will insist on a "right and wrong" approach to this situation, but it isn't that way. Balance is so important and to remember to encourage and love those around us.

HOLINESS AND POWER

Though they ought to, holiness and power do not necessarily go together. But like the old Reese's commercial about chocolate and peanut butter, *it's better when they're together.* There is a unique ugliness in a carnal Christian moving in the power of the Holy Spirit. There is also a needless helplessness in a Christian who walks with the Lord, but doesn't believe Christ has given gifts to His church. This is just one reason it is so important for people of integrity to walk in the power of the Holy Spirit and not leave the field open to charlatans.

God will use whoever is available, and if no one is, then we will use the rocks because He loves people and is so anxious to heal people. Holiness and power are like two wings on an airplane—we are meant to have both. You can have one without the other, but you can never get off the ground. This is a shame, because God meant us to fly! We are called to demystify the gifts of the Spirit, and we are called to put the ministry of the Holy Spirit back into the hand of the church!

The ministry of the Holy Spirit is for every man, woman and child in the body of Christ. All the gifts of the Spirit are for all of us! When everyone and anyone can heal the sick or cast out a demon or prophesy, then the danger of anyone becoming overly impressed with the 'minister' is diminished.

One of the lessons we learned early on in the Vineyard was that comfort is a thing of the past. Many people came to learn and see all that God was doing, but many also came to gawk and criticize. One of our "life" prophecies happened in the Vineyard in the early part of the 1980s where the Holy Spirit had been moving in great power. I was about to teach for the evening service when I noticed that many theologians and professors had come to check out what was going on in this gym that we met in.

> **We are called to demystify the gifts of the Spirit, and we are called to put the ministry of the Holy Spirit back into the hand of the church!**

It was probably one of the only times I began to get a bit nervous heading into a service. Just after worship a prophecy came that I believe is to this day for us in the Vineyard. The Lord said, "I have given you your reputation, and I can take it away." I knew this was true. I repented and continued to "do the stuff" Jesus does through us.

As we speak Jesus' words and do Jesus' works, we are to equip and train others in the process, giving away all that we have learned and continue to learn along the way. The message of Jesus is the Word and works accompanied by the power of the Holy Spirit. It gets 'em every time!

GOD'S APPOINTMENT BOOK

It had been a long day at the office, full of deadlines and meetings that leave editors eager for only one thing: getting home and relaxing with their families. As Kerry Jennings (not his real name) navigated across the freeway system toward his suburban home, he fell into prayer. He had developed this habit to redeem the hours spent in traffic jams. He interceded for his family, his co-workers, and his friends.

Then he began asking God to provide opportunities for personal evangelism. Suddenly, strange thoughts entered his mind, as well as the accompanying peace indicating the Lord was responding to his prayers. He had acted on these kinds of thoughts before, usually seeing God word through him. God told Kerry to stop at a familiar restaurant, look for a certain waitress and tell her, "God had something for her." Further, God said He would reveal what He had for the waitress when Kerry talked with her. Though apprehensive, Kerry responded to the instruction, steering his car toward the restaurant.

He did so because he sensed that God had arranged a divine appointment. A divine appointment is an appointed time in which God reveals Himself to an individual or group through spiritual gifts or other supernatural phenomena. God arranges these encounters—they are meetings He has ordained to demonstrate His Kingdom.

After being seated in the waitress' section, Kerry began to ponder all the reasons for not delivering the message. While caught up in his anxious thoughts, she approached. Before he could say anything, she cheerfully said, "You have something for me, don't you?" In response he told her that God had sent him specifically with something, and then the two insights concerning her job and a relationship (both areas of trouble for her) were supernaturally revealed to him. Asking God for courage, he told her.

She was stunned. She knew that she was encountering God because there was no way Kerry could know those things about her. Scripture calls this a word of knowledge or "message of knowledge" (see 1 Corinthians 12:8). At the end of the conversation they prayed. She cried. Later Kerry learned she was the daughter of a Christian pastor, now deceased, and that she had turned away from God. Soon after the divine appointment, she gave her heart to God.

Divine appointments are an integral part of power evangelism. People who would rather otherwise resist hearing the Gospel are instantly open to God's Word.

DIVINE PROMPTINGS

Always be prepared to give an answer to everyone who asks you to give the reason for the hope you have.

– 1 Peter 3:15

Every Christian should always be ready to proclaim the way of salvation. Yet what I described in divine appointments goes beyond the simple explanation of the Gospel. While proclamation is an important element of divine appointments, it would be misleading to think of them only as opportunities to explain the way of salvation.

For example, in Luke 19:1-10, we find the story of Jesus coming through the town of Jericho. His encounter with Zacchaeus, the short and unpopular tax collector, is an excellent illustration of a divine appointment. On seeing him, Jesus said, "Zacchaeus, come down immediately. Today I must stay at your house." Then Zacchaeus said, "Look, Lord! Here and now I give half of my possessions to the poor, and if I have cheated anybody out of anything, I will pay back four times the amount." What could explain Zacchaeus' remarkable response to such a simple request?

First, Jesus called him by name. There is no indication in Scripture that Jesus had any prior knowledge of Zacchaeus. Jesus was doing here what the Holy Spirit enables Christians to do through a word of knowledge.

Second, the townspeople hated Zacchaeus; as a tax collector he took from the Jews on behalf of the Romans, keeping everything that exceeded the Roman requirements. He was a man who probably had few friends. He yearned for acceptance and human companionship. Jesus reached out to him and communicated through a simple request for hospitality that He loved and accepted him.

Supernatural revelation—the meeting of a deep human need. It is small wonder that Zacchaeus was saved, that all resistance to the Gospel was overcome. He climbed the tree to see Jesus more clearly, but in doing so he was more clearly seen by God.

GOD REVEALING PEOPLE'S SECRETS

The gifts may operate in any setting, any time, any place. I will illustrate this with two stories, one from my own experience, and another from a young man in our church. This young man was in Huntington Beach, California, and walked by a bar that is frequented by motorcycle bikers. A biker walked out of the bar past the young man toward his motorcycle. As he passed, the Holy Spirit revealed to the young man the biker's sins and fears. So he approached the biker and described these things to him. The biker began sobbing and turned to Christ right there, in front of all his friends. He is now in our church.

We've had numerous situations like this where God has revealed people's sins either through a word of knowledge or a combination of that and a word of wisdom or prophecy. For example, I was once on an airplane when I turned and looked at the passenger across the aisle to see the word "adultery" written across his face in big letters. The letters, of course, were only perceptible to spiritual eyes. He caught me looking at him (gaping might be more descriptive) and said, "What do you want?" As he asked that a woman's name came clearly into my mind. I leaned over the aisle and asked him if the name meant anything to him. His face turned white, and he asked if he could talk to me.

It was a large plane with a bar, so we went in there to talk. On the way the Lord spoke to me again, saying, "Tell him to turn from his adulterous affair or I am going to take him." When we got to the bar I told him that God had told me that he was committing adultery, the name of the woman, and that God would take him if he did not cease. He just melted on the spot and asked what he should do. I led him through the prayer of repentance and he received Christ right there. This was in front of the stewardess and two other passengers who were shocked but then also began to cry.

My point in telling you this is that spiritual gifts can be the main generator for all kinds of evangelism, yet there is not a single evangelistic training method of which I know that teaches this. I know of no one who has written, "Ask God to show you the secret sins of people's hearts." But we do it all the time at church, and it should be the norm in our Christian walk.

Twelve

Revival and Renewal

"LETTING GOD BE GOD"

I can often remember many times when John would talk to us about the ministry of the Holy Spirit. At this time, when some of the pastors were teaching on the possible meanings of apparent signs of the Holy Spirit, John would often say, "Stick to the main and the plain," meaning don't teach on controversial things that are theory or the latest "spiritual" fad, but on the main and the plain of the Scriptures. Subjects of biblical depth: Jesus died for our sins, He rose again, and He poured out the Holy Spirit on us. Jesus Christ is God—the eternal triune God.

After a season of the Holy Spirit being poured out and different manifestations and weirdness going on in our church, John would advise Bob [Fulton] to "stick to meat and potatoes" on Sunday— the main and the plain. Too much weirdness sometimes causes a general feeling of instability. He encouraged us to emulate the apostle Paul, who said, "My message is Jesus Christ crucified." I think of that scripture when I think of the main and the plain and not getting uptight about other differences that could divide. You know, one of the Vineyard Churches in London does baby baptisms and John encouraged them because it was something that was so important to those coming from Anglican backgrounds. Even so, the teaching was always on the main and the plain.

Penny Fulton and her husband, Bob, were with John and Carol and the Vineyard since the beginning. They currently reside in Yorba Linda, California and attend the Vineyard Anaheim where they also work with the young adults and missions.

———◆———

Our first conference with John Wimber in the Netherlands was in Zwolle in 1991. The last day of the conference, John wanted to have lunch with me in town. It is my first private meeting with him. When I pick a café to have coffee and sandwiches, he refuses to go there. I was unsure why, but later found out John thought they only served beer there. So, John picked another place for us to meet. I'm not sure exactly how it went, but I said something like, "I am having problems ever since I first listened to you, but I do not regret listening to you." John started crying. Years later he reminded me of this and said it was the moment he began to love me.

When we drove back to the conference venue, we agreed that he would hand the microphone over to me at the end of the session to make any final announcements. As chairman of the conference, I wanted an opportunity to thank him and his team. After he finished his last teaching, he asked me to come to the platform. While I was walking from my seat on the front row to the platform, John said, "Come, Holy Spirit," and he walked off. So, I stood there wanting to close the conference, and thank him, but all heaven breaks loose. Before I knew it, there is an intense ministry time going on. It was the best thing that could have happened. When I went to thank John, he was nowhere to be seen. He let Jesus steal the show!

Jan Bernard Struik is the pastor of Vineyard Utrecht and National Director Vineyard Benelux.

———◆———

O ne of the basic goals I had in mind when this whole thing started, early on in the Vineyard movement, was this: "What would God do if we gave Him the chance?" What if fear or self-interest didn't restrict us? What if the need for control didn't overwhelm us? What would God do? If our own ministries were not the most important issue, what would it be like? If "church" wasn't all about us, our place, and our ways, but instead was about Jesus and what He wanted to do here on earth, what would He reveal of His heart? What if it didn't matter to us at all what was said about us—good or bad—and the only opinion that mattered was Jesus'? What would it be like?

What if we loved what Jesus loved? What if we let God be God and we just be His people? What if self-protection was not the issue, and we didn't care about looking foolish? What would God do?

Don't you want to know? Don't you want to find out? We only have these few short years to make these decisions of self-sacrifice and faith. Then the consummation of the ages will arrive, and it will be too late (see Revelation 22:11-12). I pray that the Vineyard—and all churches who have a heart to seek and respond to God—would become supple in the hands of our loving Father.

WHEN THE SPIRIT OF GOD MOVES ...

In Luke 11:13, Jesus says, "If you then, though you are evil, know how to give good gifts to your children, how much more will your Father in heaven give the Holy Spirit to those who ask him!"

After the Spirit of God visited us in the middle of the 1990s, we held a conference themed "Let the Fire Fall." It was after this time we received more letters, phone calls, and interactions than we ever had previously. As the Spirit moved and increased, we had both positive and negative responses. I think it's important to look at what is happening when God is moving and respond to the questions.

Take the birth of a baby as an example. This is usually one of the happiest events in a family's life. There are all sorts of experiences and phenomena leading up to that event. There was the conception, the preparation, the labor pains, and the birthing itself. But we don't focus on the experiences that accompany the new baby; the focus is on the baby! We don't photograph the conception, or all the preparations of the doctor's visits, or the labor, all the blood and the birth. Once that baby comes out, we photograph the baby! We talk about the baby, the product of all the experience. We celebrate the baby.

Most people love babies, but they don't necessarily like the details of the birthing process. The birthing of a child is a messy experience at best. Not many people want to hear about that part. The same thing applies to revival. We love to read and hear about revival, but going through the birthing process of revival is very much like the birthing of a child: messy. And revival can bring all kinds of reactions, some which are positive, and some which are negative. It's not necessary to explain everything connected with revival any more than a young mother needs to share in detail the travail of the birthing process. All she has to do is hold that baby up and everyone shares in the joy.

I think it's important not to evaluate a move of God too soon—in the beginning stages. We have the challenge of evaluating something that we are participating in as well as observing. Nevertheless, we assess this from both biblical criteria and from objective understanding of our experience. That doesn't mean experience carries the same weight as the Word of God.

> **Look for the fruit. Fruit takes time to grow and time to see what something will become over time.**

However, experience, church history, and tradition (to a certain degree) are undoubtedly lenses through which we view life. Church history helps illustrate how other godly people have interacted with the Scriptures while trying to discern the activity of the Holy Spirit around them. As we relate to Christians, there are things we've learned, and that understanding acts as a foundation for evaluating what happens to us.

Scripture uses the idea of fruit as a way of evaluating spiritual teaching. Jesus told how to recognize false prophets in Matthew 7:16: "By their fruit you will recognize them. Do people pick grapes from thorn bushes, or figs from thistles?" Jesus was teach-

ing that any evaluation must go beyond initial expressions, or out-
ward appearances. Look for the fruit. Fruit takes time to grow and
time to see what something will become over time. In Southern
California you can find apples on the tree in July, but they won't
be ready to eat until October.

We must not react too quickly or in some way unjustly. Merely
because what we're seeing doesn't fit our particular understanding. Gamaliel used the same "wait and see" approach in the Acts
5 when debating the Sanhedrin over what to do with the apostles
who had disregarded the gag order to stop teaching in the name
of Jesus. The Sanhedrin were on the verge of killing Peter and the
other apostles. Gamaliel stepped in to offer his wise advice:

> *Leave these men alone! Let them go! For if their purpose*
> *or activity is of human origin, it will fail. But if it is from*
> *God, you will not be able to stop these men; you will only find*
> *yourselves fighting against God.*
>
> *– Acts 5:38-39*

Spiritual reality is found in the illustration of a balanced attitude
toward unusual spiritual reality (see Acts 11:17). In Acts 10, Peter
preached the Gospel of Christ in the house of Cornelius, a
Gentile. Remember, it took an angelic visit, a vision, and the voice
of the Holy Spirit to get Peter to this divine appointment. Peter,
a Jew, was way beyond his comfort zone just being in the house
of a Roman centurion.

When he found a large gathering of people there, he began
preaching. Before Peter could finish his sermon, "the Holy Spirit
came on all who heard the message" (Acts 10:44). God shook
things up. They began speaking in tongues and praising God, in
essence a repeat of what happened in Jerusalem on the day of
Pentecost. Peter made the connection between what he saw and
something Jesus said: "John baptized with water, but you will be

baptized with the Holy Spirit" (Acts 11:16; 1:5).

How was the news of this mighty visitation of God's Spirit received by the apostles and other believers in Judea? With criticism! The church hadn't yet developed a theological grid for understanding what had happened at Cornelius' house.

Didn't the prophet Joel say God would pour out His Spirit on all people? Even though he may have not fully understood it—even though he may not have even liked it—Peter defused the anti-Gentile prejudice in Jerusalem by saying, "So if God gave them the same gift as he gave us, who believed in the Lord Jesus Christ, who was I to think I could oppose God?" (Acts 11:17).

God sometimes offends our intellect and our sense of property (see John 6:53). But that's all right because He is God. Peter in effect is saying, "Guys, I know this isn't the way we would have done this. But we're not in charge, God is. He filled these people with the Spirit. He touched them in the same way that he touched us. Let's see what God wants to do next, and by all means let's not condemn this. Let's not let our prejudices blind us to God's work. Let's wait and see what the fruit will be."

> God sometimes offends our intellect and our sense of property. But that's all right because He is God.

As we evaluate a time of renewal, we should realize that little happens in and through the church that's not some sort of mixture of humanity and the Holy Spirit. And we can't rule out the possibility of demonic activity either, or else why do we read in the epistles, "Test everything. Hold on to the good" (see 1 Thessalonians 5:21)? In a rich meeting time, someone may say, "Oh, that's the flesh" or "That's a demon" or "That's just people acting up" or "That's God." All those analysis might be accurate at any given time. This is why it is the role of pastoral leaders to exercise discernment and bring correction when it's needed.

Unfortunately, revival and refreshing sometimes stimulate responses that are less than 100 percent godly. Revival and refreshing come because the church is at a low ebb. The church, in spite of its avowal of biblical truth, is not experiencing that reality. God doesn't revive people who have it all together. He revives people who are hungry, thirsty, weak, naked, blind, and less than spotless.

At times of renewal, some people are reacting, or overreacting, and resisting. But it takes time to know what it's all going to become. So based on the New Testament perspective of fruit, we must always wait and look for the fruit of what happens.

During a season of renewal and revival there have always been some negative responses. By comparison they are in the minority, but nonetheless sometimes true. Some people who attended a conference when the Spirit of the Lord was very present were confused by what they saw and heard. Others felt left out because of an unspoken assumption that unless something outwardly dramatic happens, then you haven't received anything beneficial.

In the afterglow of a glorious meeting, one lady approached one of the pastors with a worried look on her face. "The only thing that happened to me," she said, "is that I have this incredible inner peace and joy." So the pastor reassured her that she shouldn't feel left out if the only immediate by-product is a sense of peace and joy. That's the fruit of the Spirit. Other participants at times felt used or abused by overzealous ministry on the part of some. This obviously needs correction because we want people to receive ministry in a loving, affirming, biblically sound way. Nonetheless, it's the way some people are when they are excited, touched, and moved.

In the excitement of the infilling and empowering, and moving of the Spirit, some people momentarily do things they really ought not to do. They say or do things that they think are in vogue, like "fall, fall, fall…. or "Roar, roar, roar…" Frankly, that zeal is excusable—at times—but the methodology of the ministry to one another needs correction.

As a pastor I have an obligation to bring correction to our teams at our church and to those that minister, but we also have a responsibility to interact with those who have had, for one reason or another, a negative experience.

Most of what we have experienced in renewal time in our meetings has been of God. *But it's God in humans. I trust God entirely—it's human beings that concern me!* That doesn't mean we have to expel every little thing that doesn't have a proof text. Sometimes we have to leave it in the file folder labeled, "I don't know." Nevertheless, when God is moving let's focus on the fruit that we can clearly demonstrate in Scripture, such as devotional life, witnessing, healing the sick, casting out demons, and feeding the poor.

Devotion to fellowship does not mean that you show up at all the potlucks. It means that your heart breaks when a brother or sister is not in the place he or she ought to be. Because we're devoted to one another, we can "rejoice with those who rejoice, and mourn with those who mourn, [and] live in harmony with one another" (Romans 12:15-16).

EXPLAINING THE UNEXPLAINABLE

I'm comfortable with the fact that people, under the excitement of a visitation from the Holy Spirit, do some far out things. Some things occur because of over zealousness, emotional disorder, or even the devil. But some also occur because of God. Most of us come to God with all that in place anyway. That's why we need sanctification. That's why the Word of God has to be worked out in us and out of us in a daily way.

We spend a lifetime sorting out the fleshly and devilish influences in our lives from the things of the Spirit, so that those things that are brought of God, and of the Spirit will be built into our lives. As the Westminster Shorter Catechism describes, through "God's free grace ... we are renewed in the whole man after the image of God, and are enabled more and more to die to sin and live unto righteousness."

So I discourage trying to pry an explanation out of the Bible for the more exotic and extra-biblical experiences of some. You won't find any Scripture that says, "Pogo your way to Jesus." But strange things like that happen from time to time. We've seen various vocal expressions of roaring, moaning, crying out or screaming. We've also seen an increase in what we might call the emotional responses: laughing and crying. Whereas many biblical characters responded emotionally to God from time to time, I don't see any place where the Scripture endorses or recommends this activity, other than it might relate to repentance. These are just some of the varied ways human beings respond to an encounter with God, so therefore they can be allowed.

SEEING OURSELVES CLEARLY

One of the things that did happen to me personally when revival took place in the 1990s was something that I felt led to confess to the Anaheim Vineyard, the congregation I was pastoring at the time. It was not long, just during this season of renewal that I had developed a new sensitivity to my tongue. I became acutely aware of impurity in my heart and words. I had to avoid certain subjects, and I resisted the temptation to exaggerate. I felt the negative power of my words when they impacted others. As a result, I found myself monitoring my interactions with people at a more conscientious level. On the one hand, the season of renewal caused me to be overwhelmed with the sense of God's presence and His holiness, and on the other hand, I was overwhelmed with my lack of holiness.

In the late 1970s, two West African men came to visit us at Anaheim. They had been converted to Christ a couple of years before in the revival that swept over that portion of the world following the World War II. We were impressed by the spiritual quality of these men. At one point, my wife, Carol, asked how the revival began. She and I had heard stories of healings, deliverances and many signs and wonders. We expected that some dramatic miracle had triggered this widespread move of God.

He responded that indeed it did start with a mighty work of the Holy Spirit. We couldn't wait to hear what. Carol told me later that she pictured someone being raised from the dead or something equally stunning. Instead he replied, "God showed me my sin." We were overwhelmed by the answer. I remember thinking later, *What greater work than being shown your sin!*

This is actually the normal Christian response to meeting with God. When He draws near, we suddenly see ourselves as people with unclean lips and hands in a way that we didn't when the light wasn't so bright or near.

When revival or renewal take place all sorts of things can happen. One of which are phenomenon commonly called "manifestations." Neither the Bible nor I equate phenomena such as falling, shaking, crying out, laughing or making animal noises as an experience with God. However, you can have an experience with God that may result in some of those responses.

So when I pray for someone I don't say "shake," "fall," or "roar." I've never prayed for anybody to do anything else except to get closer to God, get filled with the Spirit, get touched by God, get blessed, come into greater belief—things that are clearly defined in Scripture.

I want the experience of God's blessing to be as sovereign as it possibly can be with the proviso that God is using human instruments. Most of us have had encounters with God at the hands of other people. Someone told me about Jesus. Someone prayed for me to receive Christ. Someone else laid hands on me at a given time to be baptized with the Spirit.

One of the problems with human instruments is that quite often the human explanations are inadequate to the experience. In my case, I was converted at one point, and I was baptized in the Spirit at another point. Later someone tried to explain the scriptural concurrence to me, but, for a time, I saw these works of God as sequential.

But when I started studying the New Testament, I saw individuals getting it all at once. In time, my understanding of Scripture tempered the explanations I had been given. Not every experience will yield an explanation. Some things are a mystery because there is much about God that we don't understand.

> **When He draws near, we suddenly see ourselves as people with unclean lips and hands in a way that we didn't when the light wasn't so bright or near.**

For my thoughts are not your thoughts, neither are your ways my ways declares the Lord.

–Isaiah 55:8

I see these unusual experiences as one of many means to get where we want to go in our walk with Christ. For Peter, James, and John, seeing Jesus transfigured on the mountain into His glorified state was an awesome experience with few parallels. Their natural tendency was to build some monuments to the experience. In Matthew 17:5 God interjects by saying, "This is my Son, whom I love and am well pleased." This is the test of all renewal experiences—we need to direct our eyes and ears to God's Son, Jesus.

So my question to someone after they've shaken, fallen down, or made a noise is this: "Do you love Jesus more? Do you believe in Him more? Are you more committed to Him?" If the answer is "Yes!" then praise the Lord!

THE PURPOSE IS JESUS

When spiritual experience happens, the truth is we are happy for it. But what comes after the experience? The focus must be the product of the experience, not the experience itself.

To celebrate the accompanying experiences is to miss the point. What God allows or takes a person through is fine if it's going to result in new life; it's important to keep our focus on Jesus and His heart. What did the encounter with the Spirit of God produce? Talk about that! A healing? Great! A deliverance from a demon? Great! A new sense of God's love and compassion for you? Wonderful!

Those are the things we're supposed to be talking about. All of those things bring glory to Jesus, but the process you went through, the accompanying phenomena is beside the point. The Holy Spirit is real and we rejoice. The Spirit is God. Our message must be the same no matter what is happening as the message of life encounters our bodies. We stick with the apostles' teaching, the Gospel of Jesus Christ, and the main and the plain of the Scriptures.

If stuff happens, it happens! We don't need to explain it or apologize for it; we also don't need to advertise it or teach it. An important value we discovered is that we have a lot of room to make mistakes and learn. All of us will make mistakes when we learn to walk out what we believe. There has to be the freedom to investigate new moves of God and be a part and learn from them.

That's the way I want it to be. In fact, it would be tragic to me if the Vineyard drew back into a safe place where there was no chance for error. Don't ever stop taking risks. Whatever community of faith you are with, allow the Lord to do what He wants to and through you.

The purpose, of having a spiritual encounter is always more of Jesus. Not what we may look like, not all that may be happening all around us—we want *Him*! And when Jesus chooses to move among us, our heart stance should be, "More of You, Jesus. We want more of You."

NOTES

NOTES

NOTES

NOTES